THE DREAM WALKER

THE DREAM WALKER

Just Walk It

Venugopal Chettier

PARTRIDGE

Print information available on the last page.

To order additional copies of this book, contact
Toll Free 800 101 2657 (Singapore)
Toll Free 1 800 81 7340 (Malaysia)
orders.singapore@partridgepublishing.com

www.partridgepublishing.com/singapore

CONTENTS

To the four ladies who have played pivotal roles in various phases of my life: my mother, Neelambal, whose love, affection, and faith in me guided me through tough times; my wife, Vasugi, whose love, belief, and faith in me gave me the strength to persevere; and my daughters, Sankaree and Kavithaa, whose love, concern, and faith strengthened my resilience.

Thank you.

ACKNOWLEDGEMENTS

First of all, I would like to express my gratitude and love to my creator for giving me the guidance and flow of thoughts to put this book together.

Second, I would like to thank all the great leaders, achievers, visionaries, teachers, authors, and speakers who thought their thoughts and wrote their books and have motivated me to produce this contribution of mine.

Third, I would like to thank my daughter Kavithaa for reading the chapters and giving me her honest feedback. That boosted my confidence to stay focused and continue.

Fourth, I would like to thank Namasivayam Muniandy, retired high school principal and passionate reader, who combed through my materials to correct the language and contents. His great contribution as an exemplary professional teacher earned him the prestigious and distinguished Tokoh Guru Negeri Melaka award from the education department in the state of Malacca, Malaysia, in 2013.

Finally, I would like to thank the team at Partridge that worked closely with me to ensure a quality book reaches the reader, *you*.

INTRODUCTION

As a seeker, I felt deeply disturbed when I was not happy with my life. I wanted change but wasn't sure how to seek it. I needed new tools for success and happiness. I did not know what to do.

I found I had neglected a habit I loved very much: reading. I decided to pursue this habit daily for thirty minutes. I got back to this habit by getting up thirty minutes earlier every morning. After a few weeks, I realized I was feeling better. I decided to get up earlier by sixty minutes every morning. I started the day by expressing gratitude for the abundance in my life and by doing visualization, deep breathing, meditation, affirmation, motivation, reading, and journaling of my thoughts. After a couple of more weeks, I decided to get up ninety minutes earlier than I once had to add exercise and spend time with nature. Now, every morning, I spend close to 120 minutes a day on the development of my mind, body, and spirit to get me ready for the day without the disturbance of phone calls. My productivity has increased, and one of the end results is this book.

We are all seekers. It does not matter whether we realize it. We are all seeking something with or without our awareness. When we do something without awareness, we'll have difficulty getting the desired change or result. But when we do something with awareness, we can get the desired change or result fast and with ease. Awareness precedes change, which, in turn, predetermines success. So when we meet somebody successful, let us not assume the person is lucky. Success is actually premeditated and does not happen by luck or chance. When we accept this truth, we are destined to live a bountiful life. Mankind has developed phenomenally in the last two hundred years due to awareness. In the next one hundred years, mankind may develop in mind-boggling ways due to awareness.

We are blessed with the most powerful tool: the mind. Whatever we seek is within us. We have to tap into the unlimited potential within us to enjoy the bountiful waiting for us. I am confident this book will give you insight into this unlimited potential. We have to examine who we are, where we are going, and who we can be. We must have clarity about our purpose for being on this planet. Purpose creates passion. When we are passionate, we will take action, move towards our destiny, and live our dream life.

We do not have to reinvent the wheel. The people who came before us did what needed to be done. We just have to learn the secret to our potential from these great leaders, achievers, and visionaries. In this book, I have incorporated some of these leaders', achievers', and visionaries' thoughts to establish clarity and proof for readers. These people have laid out the key principles for us to follow. Our job is to identify these principles and follow them. It is in our hands – will we enjoy life's abundance with a teaspoon, a dipper, or a bucket?

After saying all this, I must admit I am like most of you, a work in progress. Every day, I struggle with my own limitations and fears. To fulfil my expectations, I have to challenge myself to take action while remaining motivated and excited. From when I started on this new journey, my belief in myself has multiplied many folds. I have discovered I have many choices to choose from. I have clarity when I make choices. One of the choices I made was to write this self-development book.

Thank you for choosing this book. To get the best results, I suggest you read through the book in its entirety the first time. Then highlight the pertinent points during the second reading for easy reference. If your interest persists and time permits, you should make a summary after each chapter during your third reading.

I started as a seeker. I hope and wish that you discover what you seek.

CHAPTER 1

Dreams

The journey of a thousand miles begins with a single step.

—Lao Tzu

PUSHING THE ENVELOPE

In the airline industry, *pushing the envelope* describes the mindset of a pilot who seeks to test the upper and lower limits of safety to fly at a certain speed, engine power, manoeuvrability, wind speed, or altitude. It's a personal challenge designed to determine just how far it is safe to go.

You have the choice of making things happen or letting things happen; you have the choice of setting goals to realize your dreams or letting things happen as they come. Isn't it best to commit, take your best shot, and let life do the rest? Are you ready to push the envelope to begin your journey?

WHAT IS YOUR IDEA OF HAPPINESS?

Is it being in great health, owning your dream house, having a fat bank account, travelling the world, visiting exotic places, owning your dream car, getting to know your loved ones better and spending

1

precious time with them, advancing to a new level in your career, being spiritual, or serving the society you live in? Other areas of life may be special to you as well.

Wouldn't it be wonderful if you could focus on all areas, spend time developing all areas, and enjoy the fruits of your achievement? Wouldn't it be wonderful to leave something behind that could outlast you? Wouldn't it be wonderful to leave a legacy? Wouldn't it be great to make a difference and impact others' lives? What mark of your presence would you like to leave for your loved ones, your friends, your social group, your society, or the world at large?

You might have tried hard at something that just did not work. Maybe you were not ready; maybe your timing was not correct; maybe you gave up too early. Or maybe something better is waiting for you. Just let go! Believe that bigger, better, and bolder opportunities are waiting for you to push the envelope too!

> Know thyself.
>
> —Socrates

Knowing ourselves is the secret to living with abundance in this world. *Abundance* does not refer to money alone. In whichever area we choose to focus on, we can achieve abundance – in money, education, family, career, spirit, society, or business. Just name it. The key to success is our thoughts. Our thoughts are potent when they mix with a definite purpose, persistence, and a burning desire. Successful people don't give excuses. People who give excuses, fear change, fear the unknown, and fear failure inevitably also fear success. If we want results, let's fight fear. Let's stop giving excuses.

Knowing ourselves includes knowing we were born to take risks without fear. The world around us has shaped our reality, and that includes our fears. Wanting to conform with the people with whom we interact, including our parents and loved ones, makes us model these people's habits. This can result in limiting beliefs and false assumptions. These develop over time. We wanted our parents to love us and adore us; this craving made us do things to please them.

Who you are today is who you have become by assimilating the actions and words of the people around you. If that is the case, are you really the *true you*? If you want to be the true you, you have to rescript the *real you*. You can then enjoy the bounty that awaits you.

Everything begins with our belief system. If our belief system is unshakable, nothing can deter us from reaching our goals.

> If I have the belief that I can do it, I shall surely acquire the capacity to do it even if I may not have it at the beginning.
>
> —Gandhi

If we can add the catalyst of enthusiasm to our belief system and start taking action, it will work wonders. In the process, we will identify the tools required to achieve our goals. We then learn to work within a time frame.

Just remember the power of the *BEAST*:

- Belief
- Enthusiasm
- Action
- Skill
- Time

We all tend to spend a lot of energy and time on unproductive and trivial matters. This siphons our time, which is an important ingredient for our success. If we take a little time to study the time we spend on unproductive and trivial things, we will realize its value. For things to change, we must change. As Goethe said, 'Things which matter most must never be at the mercy of things which matter least.'

The eleventh president of India, A. P. J. Abdul Kalam (1931–2015), was a professor, author, aeronautical engineer, and distinguished scientist of India. In his book *My Journey*, he writes, 'The most important lesson I have learnt is, one must keep dreaming at various phases of life, and then work hard to realize those dreams. If we do so, then success is imminent.' He also shares, 'Dreams are not those that we see in our sleep; they should be the ones that never let us sleep.'

A bachelor and a great visionary, Abdul Kalam remains one of the most distinguished scientists of India. He holds the unique honour of receiving honorary doctorates from forty universities and institutions. He died at the age of eighty-three on 27 July 2015, leaving behind 2,500 books, which were the only gifts he would accept; the rest were returned politely. During his tenure as the president of India, all the gifts foreign governments gave him were duly transferred to the Indian government, including his personal wristwatch, six shirts, four pairs of trousers, three suits, and a pair of shoes as the final savings and prized possessions. The 'Missile Man of India' did not even own a television set. He was always averse to watching television, citing that the 'idiot box' was nothing but a waste of time. A great statesman and visionary, he met and interacted with more than six million youth in the last two decades of his life. He dreamed of big achievements for his nation and its people, but not vast possessions for himself. This great statesman knew that knowing yourself is the secret to living with abundance in this world.

He shared, 'The mind is unbelievably elastic. It can expand as much as you let it, and once it opens up, there are no barriers – the belief in yourself that comes as a result is something no one can take away from you.' So when we dream, we are test pilots, forcing ourselves to push beyond our expectations. Once we do this, we are born again with new vision.

Napoleon Hill is the author of one of the most influential books of all time, *Think and Grow Rich*. In it, he points out the way to personal achievement, financial independence, and riches of the spirit beyond measurement in money. He writes, 'Whatever the mind can conceive and believe, it can achieve.'

When we repeat a thought over and over, it becomes our belief and our truth. Over time, we buy into the false thoughts the people around us teach us. These siphon and subdue the natural genius and creative giant within us. As Napoleon Hill says, 'If you want new results, just change your thought and keep repeating to form your new belief and your new truth.' The quality of our thinking determines the quality of our lives. What we decide to think and focus on determines our destiny.

In 1994, Jeff Bezos quit a lucrative job, moved to Seattle, and targeted the untapped potential of the Internet market by opening an online bookstore. He set up an office in his garage with a few employees to develop software. They expanded into a two-bedroom house equipped with three microstations. Eventually, they developed a test site. After inviting three hundred friends to beta test the site, Bezos opened Amazon.com, and within thirty days, he was selling books (written in forty-five languages) across the United States and internationally. Today, the man hailed as the king of Internet commerce runs a global powerhouse that reached US\$7 billion in sales last year. Bezos said, 'I knew that if I failed, I wouldn't regret that, but I knew that one thing I might regret is not trying.'

Seth Godin is the author of eighteen international bestsellers. His books have been translated into more than thirty-five languages and have changed the way people think about marketing and work. Godin

writes, 'The only thing worse than starting something and failing ...
is not starting something.'

We need dreams to grow – if possible, big dreams. We can face bigger
challenges. To focus on our goals, we need to change our vocabulary.
With a new mindset, our obstacles will look small and surpassable.
We should keep our eyes on our dreams and keep moving with the
Dream Walkers. We will belong to this select group of dreamers who
are making a difference in this world. Og Mandino, the author of *The
Greatest Salesman in the World*, shares, 'Failure is man's inability to
reach his goals in life, whatever they may be.'

Now let me share the story of Helen Keller, who was born in 1880.
When she was eighteen months old, she fell ill and was struck blind,
deaf, and mute. As she grew, Keller became very wild and unruly.
She inflicted raging tantrums on her parents. Her mother, desperate
for answers and inspiration, came across the story of the successful
education of Laura Bridgman, another deaf and blind child. Laura's
story was featured in *American Notes*, a travelogue written by Charles
Dickens. The child was taken to Baltimore, Maryland, to see Dr
J. Julian Chisolm. After examination, the doctor referred the child
to the inventor of the telephone, Alexander Graham Bell. Bell, in
turn, suggested they travel to Perkins School for the Blind in Boston,
Massachusetts. That is where Keller met teacher Anne Sullivan, and
that was the beginning of a relationship that lasted forty-nine years.

At first, Keller was curious and defiant. She refused to cooperate
with Sullivan's instruction. As Keller's frustration grew, the tantrums
increased. Finally, Sullivan demanded isolation with Keller. They
moved to a cottage on the Keller family's cotton plantation.

In a dramatic struggle, Sullivan taught Keller the word *water*. She
helped her make the connection between the object and the first
letter by taking Keller out to a water pump and placing Keller's hand

under the spout. When Sullivan moved the lever to flush cool water over Keller's hand, she spelled out the word *water* on Helen's other hand. Keller understood and repeated the word in Sullivan's hand. By nightfall, she had learned thirty words. As Kalam said, 'The mind is unbelievably elastic. It can expand as much as you let it, and once it opens up, there are no barriers – the belief in yourself that comes as a result is something no one can take away from you.'

In 1890, Keller began speech classes at the Horace Mann School for the Deaf in Boston. For the next twenty years, she toiled to learn to speak so that others could understand her. In 1896, she attended the Cambridge School for Young Ladies, a preparatory school for women. Henry H. Rogers, a Standard Oil executive, was so impressed with Keller's talent, drive, and determination that he agreed to pay for her to attend Radcliffe College. Keller mastered several methods of communication, including touch lip reading, Braille speech, typing, and finger spelling. While in college, she wrote her first book, *The Story of My Life*, with the help of Sullivan and Sullivan's future husband. It covered her transformation from a child to a twenty-one-year-old college student. In 1904, Keller graduated from Radcliffe College at the age of twenty-four.

In 1946, Keller was appointed counsellor of international relations for the American Foundation for Overseas Blind. Between 1946 and 1957, she travelled to thirty-six countries on five continents. In 1955, at age seventy-five, Keller embarked on the longest and most gruelling trip of her life: a forty-thousand-mile, five-month trek across Asia. Through her many speeches and appearances, she brought inspiration and encouragement to millions of people.

During her lifetime, Keller received many honours in recognition of her accomplishments. She died in 1968, just a few weeks before her eighty-eighth birthday. Keller stood as a powerful example of how determination, hard work, and imagination can allow an individual to triumph over adversity. By overcoming difficult conditions with a great deal of persistence, she grew into a respected and world-renowned activist who laboured for the betterment of others. A great visionary, Helen Keller shares a beautiful quote with us: 'The only thing worse than being blind is having sight but no vision.'

Helen Keller was a Dream Walker who lived amid many Dream Talkers. She dreamed of a better world for the deaf, blind, and mute. She was a beacon of light for the many without sight.

Helen Keller, the Dream Walker, might not have achieved what she achieved without another Dream Walker: Anne Sullivan Macy, born in 1866 to unskilled, illiterate, and impoverished immigrants from Ireland. When she was only eight years old, she contracted a bacterial eye disease that created painful infections and, over time, made her nearly blind. At that time, her mother died, and her father abandoned her brother and her for fear he could not raise them on his own. They were sent to a home, where her brother died within three months due to a hip ailment. She had an eye operation that offered some short-term relief. Then she enrolled at the Perkins School for the Blind in Boston. During that period, she had a series of eye operations that significantly improved her vision.

In 1886, at the age of twenty, she graduated. A year later, she was assigned the job to teach Helen Keller. In 1932, Keller and Sullivan were each awarded an honorary fellowships from the Educational Institute of Scotland. They were also awarded honorary degree from Temple University. In 1955, Sullivan was awarded an honorary degree from Harvard University. When she died in 1936, Sullivan was cremated, and her ashes were interred in a memorial at National Cathedral in Washington, DC. She was the first woman to be recognized for her achievements in this way. When Helen Keller died in 1968, her ashes were placed in National Cathedral next to those of Anne Sullivan Macy. Let me share another beautiful quote by Helen Keller: 'Optimism is the faith that leads to achievement. Nothing can be done without hope or confidence.'

If we believe in our dreams, we should walk towards our dreams with a friend, guide, or teacher like Anne Sullivan. What we need are Dream Walkers as friends to coax us, encourage us, and believe in us to achieve our dreams. Stay away from Dream Talkers or Dream Busters, and you will definitely achieve your dreams.

Imagine you attended a fantastic motivational seminar over the weekend. You feel fully charged and ready to walk in your dreams. Then you meet an old friend on the way to work and share your excitement with the friend. The friend looks at you and says, 'Hey, dude, I have been to a few of those seminars; they do no good. You don't have the education, the money, the connections, the support, the charisma ... *blah blah blah.*' The Dream Buster has done a perfect job. Now, you are ready to evaluate yourself: *I do not have the education, the money, the connections, the support, the charisma ... How am I going to do it?* With time, your dreams are back, safe in your cocoon, waiting for another opportunity to burst out. A reality check takes over when your loved ones, your friends, and your colleagues are not supportive because you have so many unresolved day-to-day problems to take care of.

Dream Walkers live in a world of Dream Talkers and Dream Busters. They are no different from you except they believe that they can walk their dreams in spite of all the challenges they face. If you believe the challenges are nothing compared to the opportunities, you have won half the battle.

To be a Dream Walker, you should nurture and cherish your dreams. You should keep record of all your dreams in a journal. You should review your dream journal regularly. You should select your major dreams and work on them daily. You should do what it takes to make your dreams come true. You should discipline yourself to work on your dreams and make sacrifices to achieve them.

Dream Talkers spend most of their time simply surviving, losing sight of their human potential. They focus on their weaknesses and just talk about their dreams. They are not willing to discipline themselves to work towards realizing their dreams. On the other hand, Dream Walkers thrive. Focusing on their strengths gives them the best shot to succeed.

Back in the good old days in India, there was an arrow maker who made excellent arrows. He stayed busy shaping and sharpening arrowheads in his hands. To get the best result, the artisan treated every piece of work as unique and special, with his mind solely absorbed in the work at hand. The end result reflected the artisan's commitment. While the arrow maker was working one day, the king led a procession through the street past him with all pomp, splendour, and gaiety. The arrow maker stayed so focused that he was not disturbed by the gaiety. He was so detached from everything around him except his work that he did not notice what was happening around him. The great sage Dattatreya, travelling the way, observed this. He asked the arrow maker about the procession. The arrow maker was at a loss for words. Dattatreya said, 'I learned from the arrow maker the quality of intense concentration of the mind by detaching from everything else except being solely absorbed in the work in hand.'

Wouldn't it be fantastic if you could give 100 per cent of yourself to whatever you do? Whether it be the least important or the most important work, just don't lose sight of it till you complete it.

Let me share with you the true story of a child who made a difference with her fifty-seven-cent dream to have a new Sunday school class. On Sunday mornings, her Sunday school was generally crowded, and the children were greatly disturbed because they could not get in due to the crowd. One of them was little Hattie May Wiatt, who lived nearby. One morning, she stood by the gate with her books and contribution, not knowing whether to go home or wait and try to get in later. Just then, minister Russell H. Conwell saw her and lifted her onto his shoulder. She held on to his head as he carried her through the crowd, through the hall, and into the Sunday school room and seated her in a chair back in a dark corner.

The next morning, on the way to church from his home, Conwell went by Hattie's house. She was going up the street to school. As he approached her, he said, 'Hattie, we are going to have a larger Sunday school room soon.'

She said, 'I hope you will. It is so crowded that I am afraid to go there alone.'

'Well,' he replied, 'when we get the money with which to erect a school building, we are going to construct one large enough to get all the little children in, and we are going to begin very soon to raise the money for it.' This idea only existed in his mind, as a kind of imaginary vision, but he wished to make conversation with the child.

He next heard that Hattie was very sick, and they asked him to come see the child and pray with her, which he did. As he walked down the street, he prayed for the little girl's recovery, yet all the time with the conviction that it was not to be. The little girl died. After the funeral, her mother handed Russell a little bag of the fifty-seven cents gathered by the girl. He took it to the church and stated that they had the first gift toward the new Sunday school building; little Hattie May Wiatt, who had gone on into the shining world, had left behind her gift towards it. He then changed the money in for pennies and offered the pennies for sale. He received about $250 for the fifty-seven pennies, and the people who bought fifty-four of those pennies returned them to him. Two hundred fifty dollars was enough to buy the house next to the church, north at Berks and Mervine.

The crowd at the church and school got bigger, so they needed to grow the premises more. Conwell went to see Mr Baird, who lived on the corner, and asked what he wanted for the lot on which the church stood. He said that he wanted $30,000. Russell said they only had fifty-four cents toward the $30,000. When he went to meet with Mr Baird again after some time, Mr Baird said, 'I have been thinking this matter over and have made up my mind. I will sell you that lot for $25,000, taking $5,000 less than I think it is worth, and I will take the fifty-four cents as the first payment, and you may give me a mortgage for the rest at 5 per cent.' The pastor later went back, left the fifty-four cents with Mr Baird, and took a receipt for it as a partial payment on the lot. Afterwards, Mr Baird returned the fifty-four cents as another gift. At the end of the building's construction, they owned $109,000 worth of property. This is taken from a sermon by Russell H. Conwell, given on Sunday, 1 December 1912, when the picture of Hattie May Wiatt, who died in 1886, was unveiled.

The fifty-seven cents has transformed over time into Temple University in Philadelphia, Pennsylvania. Hattie's insignificant contribution has become significant. Russell H. Conwell founded the university in 1884. As of 2014, more than thirty-seven thousand undergraduate, graduate, and professional students are enrolled in more than four hundred academic-degree programs offered at seven campuses and sites in Pennsylvania and at international campuses in Rome, Tokyo, Singapore, and London.

Temple University Hospital is a general medical and surgical hospital in Philadelphia. It is a teaching hospital that has 728 beds. The hospital had 37,254 admissions in the latest year. It performed 7,679 annual inpatient and 6,108 outpatient surgeries. Its emergency room had 131,590 visits.

Extraordinary things can be achieved with faith and belief. In this case, a little girl's dream had so much energy. This little girl provided the first snowflake to create an avalanche. She acted on her dream of a bigger and better Sunday school. When Conwell shared the news with her, she immediately moved to action, saving money for the Sunday school. She did not live to see her dream realized, but she energized him to pick up momentum. Mother Teresa summed it up excellently when she spoke about how significant we are: 'We ourselves feel that what we are doing is just a drop in the ocean. But the ocean would be less because of that missing drop.'

Can you sit back, relax, and think about how significant you are? Will you enjoy your greatest gift – your mind – in a few drops on a teaspoon or a bucketful? All you seek is within you. You can make a difference.

If the ideas I share in this book fire up your dreams, moving you towards your goal, I have successfully played a small part in making you, my reader, become a Dream Walker.

You have to develop empowering new habits to prepare yourself for the opportunities waiting to greet you. You must discard old bad habits, which are the stumbling blocks to your progress. You must nurture new empowering habits to replace your old bad ones. Only a new habit can replace an old unwanted habit. You must convey your new habit to your conscious mind daily. For this to happen, I have captured the key thoughts as *power thoughts*.

Read the power thoughts three times a day for the next thirty days to form new habits. You should do the first reading when you rise in the morning. Read them again in the afternoon after lunch. Finally, read them aloud at night just before you go to bed. The messages will become part of your conscious mind. Then they will seep into your mysterious and powerful subconscious mind, which creates your dreams. When you repeat the power thoughts joyfully with love, they will give birth to new habits you create consciously.

POWER THOUGHTS 1

Today, I affirm I am unique and special. I am a winner from my inception. I am the only one from my father's semen to successfully enter my mother's ovum membrane for fertilization when competing against more than 150 million sperm. I earned a place in this world when the sperm and egg combined to form a single cell: the successful me. Not another person in this universe has my DNA. Not another person in this universe has my thumbprint. Not another person in this universe has my voice. I will never compare myself to another person, as I am unique and I am special.

Today is the start of a new chapter in my life. I look forward to every second, every minute, and every hour of the day. I am a great dreamer. I nurture and cherish my dreams. I am committed to realizing my dreams. I am disciplined to achieve my dreams. I sacrifice to achieve my dreams. I enjoy my dreams.

Today onwards, I will start keeping track of all my dreams in a journal. I will review my dream journal weekly. I will select my major dreams and work on them daily.

I have a great mind. My mind is unbelievably elastic. I expand my mind as much as I want. Once my mind expands, I can break all barriers and achieve my dreams. I am a Dream Walker.

Whatever I can conceive and believe, I can achieve. I always give importance to the things that matter most to me.

When I want new results, I change my thought. When I keep repeating my new thought, it becomes my new belief and new truth.

CHAPTER 2

Legacy

Children wiser than parents give pleasure to all the
worldly beings.

—Thiruvalluvar

Renga was born in the midst of the Indian famine of 1896 into a
poor peasant family during the Madras Presidency, which put most of
southern India under the direct rule of the British Crown. His family
lived in a remote village 110 kilometres from the city of Madras, which
was the winter capital.

The famine spanned more than two years, devastating the livelihoods
of millions of farmers. There was barely enough food to provide even
a single meal to hungry mouths. Poor sanitation, deplorable living
conditions, inadequate health care, and accompanying epidemics
contributed to very high mortality rates. More than a million lives
ended as a result of the famine. For years, people suffered from
malnutrition and diseases. Devastating and horrifying memories of
the famine lingered in people's minds for years.

The after effects of the famine left deep scars on Renga's mind while
he grew up. People's sufferings resonated in his ears as he grew into a
teenager. In 1833, when the British abolished slavery, sugar and rubber
plantations in the colonies were in urgent need of manpower. Using

the kangani system of labour recruitment, the British tapped surplus manpower in South India, particularly from Madras, for their tea, coffee, and rubber plantations in Ceylon (now known as Sri Lanka) and Malaya (now known as Malaysia). Under the kangani system, they authorized Indian headmen to recruit entire families and ship them to the plantations. They licensed the recruiters and subsidized transportation to the plantations. They also recruited youngsters to work in these countries to build roads, rails, and harbours. The recruiters came with bag full of promises and fairy tales of the 'promised land'.

Renga was one of those who bought into their promises. Knowing his parents would not approve of his desire, one evening in 1912, Renga decided to ride to the city in a bullock cart to board a cargo ship and set off to the promised land with big dreams and empty pockets. After days of travelling, sleeping below deck amid the cargo, with rationed food, Renga landed in the promised land of Malaya in the port town of Penang. He was hurled into a rubber plantation with meagre food and deplorable living conditions. He was badly shaken up, but he did not lose hope. For a couple of years, he worked hard to make ends meet despite the deplorable working conditions. He waited patiently for the right time to act. He grabbed the first opportunity he got to move on with his quest for a better future in Seremban, a town three hundred kilometres away. He joined a roadworks company. There, in Seremban, he met a woman named Valliammal, fell in love with her, and married her. Then, they moved to Johor Bahru on the southern tip of Malaya.

This industrious Dream Walker couple worked laying road under the hot sun during the day and caring for their cattle after work. At the break of dawn, the wife took it upon herself to make and sell *thosai* (Indian pancakes) to the local residents to supplement their income. After work, the husband milked the cows and sold the milk to local residents and restaurants. They saved a portion of their income and banked with a grocery shop owner who served as the local banker. Over time, this savings grew, but the grocer's business went on the decline. The grocer could not continue with his business, nor return this young couple's money. The grocer offered the couple the opportunity to take over his ailing business. This couple did not have the education, the knowledge, the expertise, or the experience to run the business. They were just Dream Walkers who had big dreams, and the determination to achieve their dreams with focus and massive action.

The key to success is your thoughts. Your thoughts are potent when mixed with definite purpose, persistence, and a burning desire. These Dream Walkers didn't make excuses, fear change, fear the unknown, or fear failure. I must add that his wife, Valliammal, was a pillar of strength in their success story. The Midas touch for their success came from her. Their success story is a blend of the love, sweat, and labour of a truly remarkable couple. She had to diligently juggle her time between her family responsibilities and business commitments. Whatever money she made selling the Indian pancakes, she stashed it away safely for a rainy day, without her husband's knowledge. When they needed money to stock the shop and the thought of borrowing money to stock the shop disturbed him, Renga was taken aback when she declared that she had saved some money from her pancake business. When they counted the money, they were at a loss for words, as it amounted to a couple of thousands. With this seed money, they were able to stock the shop.

Over the years, the couple transformed the business into a thriving manufacturing and distribution hub, which served their customers and retail outlets on the nearby plantations. But when World War II reached the shores of Malaya in 1940, this couple's dreams were nearly shattered when the Japanese Imperial Army invaded Malaya. Renga was heartbroken but did not lose hope. When the impact of the war heightened, he had to make a decision to cease operations. The couple strategized; they made the shop look like it was in a gloomy, ruined, rundown, and deplorable condition by shifting all their stock to the upper floor and destroying the staircase. They moved with their family to the nearby rubber plantation. As the war progressed, the family suffered from increasingly severe rationing, hyperinflation, and lack of resources.

In September 1945, the Japanese forces in Malaya surrendered the country back to the British Empire. Then life slowly but surely returned to normal. Many families were left penniless, as the banana tree currency notes they held were now worthless. When the couple returned to their home with their family, they were left speechless; they felt blessed to see their shop as they had left it. They rebuilt the staircase, claimed the British currency they stashed away to start all over, and built the business into a thriving retail and wholesale outlet and distribution hub for the retail outlets located on the nearby plantations. They added a manufacturing unit at a nearby shop lot, which produced some of the daily consumer goods of their customers and the retail outlets on the plantations, bearing their own brand and trademark. The addition of a warehouse and a fleet of vehicles enabled the business to grow by leaps and bounds. This is the true story of my grandfather Rengasamy Chettiar and my grandmother Valliammal, who went to Malaya as immigrant workers with big dreams. They lived life as Dream Walkers, staying focused on their dreams and taking massive actions.

I'd like to share with you the little I can recollect of my grandpa when I was six years old. On Sundays, this tanned, lean, clean-shaven gentleman with large ears, striking features, and a head of white hairs would come home in a chartered private car attired in traditional white dhoti, baggy white shirt with sleeves extending beyond his biceps, and a black umbrella clasped in one fist. Occasionally, he would take me to the car, holding me by his other fist, and he would take me with him to a gathering at a religious teacher's tomb, decorated and draped in colourful cloth, ten kilometres away in Singapore, the town bordering ours. The smell of perfume and lighted, aromatic joss sticks created a mystical atmosphere. After a short prayer, the goat slaughtered for prayer was cooked and served as a meal for the congregation. The poor people residing in the vicinity enjoyed this sumptuous meal. I think my grandfather enjoyed the ritual of serving the food and felt it was his way of giving back to society.

Recently, I attended a Total Success training given by the motivational speaker, personal finance instructor, life coach, and self-help author Tony Robbins in Singapore. The seven thousand participants were mesmerized by this great speaker over two days. I wish to share one of his sayings with you: 'It is in your moments of decision your destiny is shaped.' What Tony Robbins said fitted my grandfather perfectly.

My grandfather's destiny was shaped by four critical moments in his life. The first was when he decided to beat poverty by leaving his loved ones and sailing to Malaya with the hope of reaching the promised land, a decision that gave him good results based on good judgement. The second occurred when he decided to save part of his income regularly and diligently for his family's future. He might not have understood the power of compound interest as he saved his money with the grocery shop owner, but he definitely understood that he had to save money regularly from whatever he earned. He knew the salary he was earning would not give him financial freedom, but what he did with his time after work definitely gave him financial freedom – another decision that gave him good results based on good judgement. Third, he decided to be a risk taker by taking over an ailing business and making it a thriving business – another decision that gave him good results based on good judgement. Fourth, he had the presence of mind to disguise his shop as a gloomy, ruined, rundown, and deplorable environment by stacking his products upstairs – another decision that gave him good results based on good judgement.

He lived a true Dream Walker life in a world of Dream Talkers. He made decisions that gave him good results based on good judgement at the most critical moments of his life. He was an illiterate but industrious man with limited funds, protecting the gate to his dreams with massive positive actions. The decisions you make every moment, living in the present and staying focused on what you have and what you can control, determine the quality of your life and your future. Have you given serious thought to what you want your future to be and decided how you want to get there? You will shape your destiny during your moments of decision making.

Marilyn Ferguson, the author of *The Aquarian Conspiracy*, published in 1980, said, 'No one can persuade another to change. Each of us guards a gate of change that can only be opened from the inside. We cannot open the gate of another either by argument or by emotional appeal.' Each one of us holds the master key for our change. As such, you are the only one who can persuade you to change. Don't waste your time trying to change somebody by argument or emotional appeal.

Another Dream Walker in my life was my father, Nadesan Chettiar. Born in 1927, he was the eldest in a family of five children. His parents were busy building their business as he was growing up. He grew up in a neighbourhood largely made up of labour-class Indians working for the railways and roadworks. The living conditions in the workers' quarters were deplorable, with little consideration for sanitation. The workers lived in wooden houses with big families and little to feed their loved ones. The youths were truant and in pursuit of little pleasures and a leader to lead them. He fitted into the role well and got involved in their mischievous activities. His focus shifted from his studies to his gang's activities. His parents were losing control over their son. Realizing their predicament, they packed him off to their homeland: Madras, India. In the meantime, World War II started, and they lost contact with their son for three years. He was left without money, and he had to fend for himself. He took up odd jobs, including working as a cook to feed him. Life was not easy, but it taught him the value and importance of relationships and money.

After the war, life started returning to normal. He was able to sail back to Malaya and reunite with his parents. At that point, their family business was booming; they needed additional hands to manage the manufacturing and distribution division. His return was timely for the business's expansion. He stayed actively involved in the traditional family business for fourteen years. The prosperity offered him the opportunity to venture across the causeway in Singapore to start a successful wholesale business of spices, grains, pulses, oilseeds, rice, and chillies at Market Street in Singapore. These products were imported from the rich spice-trading nations of South East Asia and the Indian subcontinent.

What you see of Market Street in Singapore today are tall, urban constructions on either side, which have gone through several changes. It is one of Singapore's oldest streets. In the late eighteenth century and early nineteenth century, it was an enclave of Indian money lenders, or *chettiars*. The shophouses, called *kittangis*, were predominantly occupied by these moneylenders. Each kittangi housed many moneylenders, who operated their businesses in small working spaces with a top-opening, raised, wooden working table that housed all the records and provided space to sit cross-legged and operate the business. The moneylenders usually slept within the confines of their business areas.

After starting the wholesale business, my father felt a need to diversify and push the envelope. The property market was booming, and it caught his attention. He got involved in land brokerage, which gave him handsome returns. With the returns, he bought fifty acres of rubber plantation near an army camp that stationed British soldiers. The soldiers wanted homes for their loved ones close to their place of work and away from the hustle and bustle of the town. He roped in a friend to develop the land into a housing estate called Majidee Park. They built more than two hundred spacious houses to suit the tastes and needs of the different ranks of soldiers. The project housed bungalows, semi-detached and terrace houses. It was not easy to find buyers, as bank loans were hard to come by, but the prospect of renting the premises to British soldiers made it easy to find people with funds to invest in the properties. Over time, the place bloomed into a vibrant housing estate, housing many British soldiers' families, and some of the local buyers invested to reside there. During Christmas, the place used to be transformed into a fairyland, with the houses brightly lit and with merrymaking into the wee hours of the morning. The investors reaped handsome returns on rentals and profits from appreciation when they sold the property years later.

In the midst of his busy business life, my father felt the need to play an active role in the business association, and he served in the chamber of commerce. His passion to serve the community got him into community service. This also led him to politics. He impacted many lives.

At this time, let me share my father's final journey. I think the best time to witness how much people love you is when you breathe your last breath. What matters is not how much you earned, how wealthy you lived, or how much you left behind; in the final analysis, it is how much you loved, how much you cared, all the good things you did for the people around you, and how they perceived you as a person. You see the faces of friends, family, and the people there; you feel the shared sorrow of losing you; and you feel the joy of their having known you that radiates from their hearts. So many people attended my father's funeral that hundreds of mourners had to stand on the street. When his cortege left, my family witnessed the spectacular, heart-wrenching final journey of a well-lived man sent off with the honour they felt he deserved. Thousands of people gathered to send off a man they loved. The procession of the flower-draped hearse was preceded by a motorcade, a march parade, solemn music by a brass band brigade, senior federal ministers, prominent leaders, and laymen walking side by side, silently.

My father, Nadesan Chettiar, the son of a first-generation migrant worker, was a Dream Walker. He was one among the few Indians involved in housing development in Malaya. He paved the way for his ethnic people to invest in real estate and reap handsome returns. He could have lived as a Dream Talker, living on his father's dream. But he pushed the envelope to pursue his dream and live as a Dream Walker. His actions as a risk taker, venturing into a new and unexplored industry that many feared and thought impossible, made it possible for him to find his edge and leave a legacy. As Tony Robbins says, 'Life is a gift, and it offers us the privilege, opportunity, and responsibility to give something back by becoming more.'

The life we live is a beautiful gift to us. This gift comes to us with privileges and opportunities to serve and live as we choose to live. If you understand this truth and believe in it, you are blessed to live a bountiful life. The more you give, the more you receive. Enjoy the privileges, opportunities, and responsibilities that come with life by giving back and receiving bountifully.

I wish to share with you an event that had a great impact on my life. My mother has diligently observed the anniversary of my father's death since 1976. It is customary for us to visit his grave to clean its surroundings before the prayer. On the morning of the thirtieth anniversary, I was at the graveyard. I wanted some help clearing the grounds. I observed a haggard-looking man in tattered clothing, uncombed hair, and unshaven, sprouting beard sitting with an empty plastic cup and an empty, cheap wine bottle, lost in his own world. I offered to pay him to clean the grave. He took the offer. As he started cleaning, he became sober, noticed the picture on the tombstone, and said, 'I know this man; he helped me.' Then he went on to share his story: 'I wanted to work in the neighbouring country, Singapore. I went to apply for my passport, but the immigration department wanted a referral. I approached many, but none helped me. This man did not know me, but he stood as a referral for me.'

As Charles Spurgeon said, 'A great character is the best tombstone. Those who loved you and were helped by you will remember when forget-me-nots have withered. Carve your name on hearts, not on marble.' Also, Mother Teresa said so passionately what all of us must etch in our hearts: 'Not all of us can do great things. But we can do small things with great love.'

Life gives us the opportunity to make decisions. Our decisions can give us good results based on good judgement or bad results based on bad judgement. In either case, the experience gained is valuable. Good results based on good judgement make us happy and make us perform better, whereas experience gained from bad results based on bad judgement makes us frustrated and unhappy. We generally blame ourselves; when we do this, our mind identifies justification to make the blame foolproof. Then we admit guilt and shut ourselves away. Stop the blame game; learn to forgive, forget, and move ahead. We should treat our experiences as lessons to take new actions.

Now ask yourself what a family member, a friend, a work colleague, and a member from your service club would say about your character, your contributions, and your achievements if they were asked to do so at your memorial after you depart. What would you want them to say? Just take a few minutes to jot that down. Now ask yourself what they would really say about you. Just take a few more minutes to jot that down. Compare both answers. Now decide what you want to do about how your two responses differ. You are a sculptor who can take a rock, chip away the unwanted parts, and create an inspiring sculpture. I wish you the best on your journey to making your greatest creation.

In chapter 1, I said to discard old bad habits, which are the stumbling blocks to your progress. You must nurture new empowering habits to replace your old bad habits. Only a new habit can replace an old unwanted habit. You must convey the new habit to your conscious mind daily. Again, l have captured the chapter's key thoughts as *power thoughts*. If you have not completed your thirty days of contemplating chapter 1's power thoughts, please combine both chapters' power thoughts, and read them three times daily for the next thirty days to form new habits. The first reading should happen when you rise in the morning. Read the power thoughts again in the afternoon after lunch. Finally, read them aloud at night just before you go to bed. The messages will become part of your conscious mind. Then they will seep into your mysterious and powerful subconscious mind, which creates your dreams. When you keep repeating them joyfully, with love, they will give birth to a new good habit, which you create consciously.

POWER THOUGHTS 2

Today, I affirm I shape my destiny when I make decisions. My past decisions have shaped my present life. The decisions I make from today will shape my future life. I am living in the present, focused on the future.

Today, I affirm I am the only person who can change myself. The gate of change can only be opened by me from the inside. The key to my success is with me. I change myself for the better and enjoy the abundance.

The beautiful life I am enjoying is a gift to me. I know this gift comes with privileges and opportunities to serve and live my life as I choose. I am aware the more I give, the more I receive. I am blessed to live a bountiful life.

My life gives me the opportunity to make decisions about my actions. I am aware my decisions can lead to good results or bad results. I am aware good results will make me happy and make me perform better. I am aware I should forgive myself for bad decisions and treat the experiences gained from bad decisions as opportunities to propel me to new actions.

I am aware I can live a great life doing small things with great love. Today onwards, I will perform even the smallest things with great love.

CHAPTER 3

Choices

Age is just a number. It's totally irrelevant unless, of course, you happen to be a bottle of wine.

—Joan Collins

COLONEL SANDERS

The mascot of every Kentucky Fried Chicken (KFC) restaurant is the sturdy, elderly gentleman Harland Sanders – with his white suit and string tie, white hair, white moustache, and white goatee – the founder of the franchise. His is a truly inspiring and amazing success story. Age had no bearing on Harland Sanders' perseverance, dedication, ambition, and hard work to create success.

At the tender age of six, in 1896, Harland Sanders had to take care of his two younger siblings after the death of his father. By the age of seven, he picked up the art of cooking and mastered many dishes. At the age of ten, he started working as a farmhand, then as a conductor, soldier, fireman, insurance salesman, and steamboat operator, and he even practised law. He worked no less than twenty-five jobs.

I think each of the failures I had to face provided me with the opportunity of starting again and trying something new.

　　　　　　　　　　　　　　　—Colonel Sanders

He ran a service station, where he started cooking for the travellers at the age of forty. The customers liked his cooking, so the patrons increased, and the crowd got better. Sanders moved across the street to a bigger place with a motel–restaurant setting to service the increased demand. At that time, he also perfected his special eleven-herbs-and-spices fried chicken recipe. A salesman approached Sanders and convinced him to invest in twelve pressure cookers to quicken his cooking process. Then he finally reached his trademark recipe.

In 1935, Sanders was made an honorary colonel by Kentucky governor Ruby Laffoon in honour of his cooking skills. Hence, he was then known as Colonel Sanders. In 1952, Colonel Sanders decided to devote himself to franchising his chicken after his restaurant business closed due to a new highway being built where his restaurant was located.

Colonel Sanders decided not to retire and live off his Social Security cheque of US$105 when he reached the age of sixty-five, saying, 'My life isn't over and I'm not going to sit in a rocking chair and take money from the government.' Colonel Sanders decided to actively franchise his special fried chicken recipe. He travelled in his car, promoting his franchise to restaurants. He even slept in the back of his car promoting his chicken. He cooked his chicken with the eleven secret herbs and spices, served it to restaurant owners, and asked only for a franchise fee of four cents for every fried chicken sold. The story goes that he was turned down 1,009 times before a restaurant accepted his special fried chicken recipe! When someone asked him about his perseverance, the colonel said, 'So many other people have strived through adversity that it will embarrass you.'

When the deal was struck, the restaurant received packets of the colonel's secret herbs-and-spices recipe. By 1964, Colonel Sanders had six hundred franchises selling his trademark fried chicken. At that time, Colonel Sanders sold his company for US$2 million but remained as the spokesman. In 1976, the Colonel was ranked the world's second most recognizable celebrity.

This is the amazing story of a Dream Walker who started at the age of sixty-five and ended up building a global empire out of fried chicken, when most people would have retired and lived as Dream Talkers. Many of us have hidden talents and don't give our dreams an opportunity to bloom. We live as Dream Talkers when we could nurture our dreams as Dream Walkers. They say actions speak louder than words. In a world filled with Dream Talkers who talk about their dreams, some people are quietly taking action to move towards their dreams. Many of us would give up after a few tries; others might try a little longer. But you seldom find many who keep going after 1,009 unsuccessful attempts. That is the reason why we still talk about Colonel Sanders.

SISTER MADONNA

Another great Dream Walker is Marie Dorothy Buder. When she was twenty-three years old, she followed her first calling in life and became a nun. More than two decades later, as Sister Madonna, she found her second calling: running. Sister Madonna began training at age forty-eight at the advice of Father John, who told her it was a way of tweaking mind, body, and spirit and bringing relaxation and calmness to an individual. She completed her first triathlon at age fifty-two and her first Ironman event at age fifty-five, and she has continued ever since.

At a time when many of her peers were slowing down, Sister Madonna was just warming up. At fifty-two, she added swimming and biking to her repertoire, and since 1982, she has breezed through more than

350 triathlons, including 45 Ironman events (which feature a 2.4-mile swim, 112-mile bike ride, and 26.2-mile run). In 1996, she completed an Ironman event in 14:27:14, fast enough to break the world record for sixty-five- to sixty-nine-year-olds. Just eight weeks after fracturing her arm in a bike collision, Sister Madonna won her age group at the USA Triathlon National Championship, proving she was as resilient as ever.

At the 2005 Hawaii Ironman, at age seventy-five, the 'Iron Nun' became the oldest woman ever to complete the race, finishing one hour before the midnight cut-off time. At the 2006 Hawaii Ironman, at age seventy-six, she again became the oldest woman ever to complete the race, finishing with a time of 16:59:03. She missed completing the 2008 Ironman triathlon in Canada. In 2009, seventy-nine-year-old Sister Madonna completed the same Ironman in 16:54:30 to become the oldest female finisher. She attempted the 2010 and 2011 Ironman Canada races, but a wetsuit issue and a missed bike cut-off time stunted her efforts.

Sister Madonna's biography was released in 2010. *The Race to Grace* tells the story of a courageous woman who broke with convention, followed her heart, and found her higher mission. In it, she says, 'Anyone can run. If you can walk, you can run. It takes no more skill than that. It comes as naturally as breathing. A lot of people are their own worst enemies.'

Eighty-four-year-old Sister Madonna Buder was not able to finish the Ironman World Championship race in Kailua-Kona, Hawaii, in 2014. At the age of eighty-four, this was quite an accomplishment, but apparently not enough for Sister Madonna. Sister Madonna still hold the record for being the oldest person to complete an Ironman race, but she wanted to make a new record as the oldest person to finish a championship Ironman race. Sister Madonna was inducted into the USA Triathlon Hall of Fame in 2014.

ABRAHAM LINCOLN

The next gentleman, called the greatest antislavery leader, also had a fair number of failures during his lifetime, despite the fact that he was a successful politician and lawyer. His failures are highlighted here to show even a failure can succeed through persistence. Many of us would have given up, but not this man.

- At the age of twenty-three, he was defeated for state legislature.
- At the age of twenty-four, he failed in business.
- At the age of twenty-six, he lost his sweetheart due to death.
- At the age of twenty-seven, he had a nervous breakdown.
- At the age of twenty-nine, he was defeated in the election for the Speaker.
- At the age of thirty-four, he was defeated in a nomination for Congress.
- At the age of forty-five, he was defeated in the election for the Senate.
- At the age of forty-seven, he was defeated in the nomination for vice president.
- At the age of forty-nine, he was defeated in the election for the Senate.

These are the failures of president Abraham Lincoln, who, at the age of fifty-one, was elected the sixteenth president of the United States of America. In his own words,

> I was born February 12, 1809, in Hardin County, Kentucky. My parents were both born in Virginia, of undistinguished families – second families, perhaps I should say. My mother, who died in my tenth year, was of a family of the name of Hanks. ... [My father] removed from Kentucky to ... Indiana, in my eighth year. ... It was a wild region, with many bears

and other wild animals still in the woods. There I
grew up. ... Of course when I came of age I did not
know much. Still somehow, I could read, write, and
cipher ... but that was all.

A self-taught lawyer who had very little formal education, he had
to work constantly to support his family, working at various jobs,
including as a shopkeeper and postmaster. Some people break when
in trouble. But failure developed Lincoln's character, gave him internal
growth, and made him bigger to break records. The sixteenth president
of the United States, Abraham Lincoln was instrumental for abolishing
slavery in the United States.

Always bear in mind that your own resolution to
succeed is more important than any other.
—Abraham Lincoln

This chapter tells true stories of Dream Walkers who had burning
desires, faith, perseverance, ambitions, dedication, and hard work.
With all these, they took massive actions to succeed. Dream Walker
Colonel Sanders gives a fitting tribute to every person who thinks
life is not done when you retire: 'I believe that you have to plan your
retirement, not by thinking that you will be deprived of something,
but rather that something will be added to your life. You see, you do
not start from zero, you are rich with the totality of experience that
life has given to you. The past years are like a crown which you wear
at the beginning of the next phase of your life.'

Colonel Sanders and Sister Madonna are classic examples of people
who have proved age has no bearing on success. At any age, you
can achieve the success you dream of. Never let others talk you into
abandoning your dreams, saying you are too old. Age is only a number;
you can erase it from your memory and enjoy your life the way you
want to.

Life is all about choices. Your destiny unfolds according to your choices. Colonel Sanders had the choice of living on Social Security or pursuing his dream to franchise his chicken recipe. Sister Madonna had the choice of serving as a nun or pursuing her dream to run. Abraham Lincoln had the choice of living as a lawyer or becoming the president of a great nation. Colonel Sanders decided to franchise his chicken, Sister Madonna decided to pursue her dream to run, and Abraham Lincoln decided to pursue his dream to be the president of the United States.

Tony Robbins says, 'It is in your moments of decision your destiny is shaped.' Colonel Sanders' destiny was shaped when he relentlessly pursued his dream. Today, there are more than eighteen thousand KFC outlets in 115 countries and territories around the world, and the number is growing. Sister Madonna's destiny was shaped when she relentlessly pursued her dream to run at the age of forty-eight. Today, Sister Madonna holds the record for being the oldest person to complete an Ironman race and is in the USA Triathlon Hall of Fame. Abraham Lincoln's destiny was shaped when he relentlessly pursued his dream to be the president of the United States despite the numerous defects he faced. Today, the world remembers him as one of the best presidents of the United States of America.

Colonel Sanders, Sister Madonna, and Abraham Lincoln were unreasonable people who followed their heart instead of the world's thoughts. All inventions, all progress, all advancements, and all discoveries came about because somebody had the courage not to listen to the crowd, like Colonel Sanders, Sister Madonna, and Abraham Lincoln. These people refused to think and act like everybody else. These people refused to get to the end of their life without living their dreams.

Learn to set goals that will put you on the mountaintop to enjoy the splendid view of your achievements. These rewards can be fantastic, but more than that is the reward of the person you become in the process of moving towards your goals. You realize the unlimited potential that has lain hidden and underutilized. This reward is far superior to achieving your actual goals. This transformation will put you on top of the world. You will start liking yourself more when your confidence level goes up. Your loved ones, your friends, and the community at large will look at you differently.

It is said that time and tide wait for no man. If you fail to plan, then you are planning to fail. Most people go to great lengths planning their holidays but give little thought to planning their lives. It is wonderful to plan your holiday, but give the same attention to your life. You feel elated sharing your wonderful experience and feelings after a great holiday. You will also feel elated when you achieve a goal you set and achieve. Your routine activities fill your days; you procrastinate and put achievement of your goals on hold. Don't let procrastination run or ruin your life. You should keep your most important goal in the forefront of your mind. Successful people take time to think, plan, and reflect from the beginning to achieve their goals. Commit to managing your time efficiently. Discipline yourself to focus on your priorities. Love your time, appreciate your time, and be stingy with your time. Don't let others steal your time. Value it as your prized possession, and invest it in activities that will give you your desired results. Whatever time you have squandered in the past is gone. You cannot do anything about it. But you can start fresh this very minute with new vigour and belief. Ask yourself if you are willing to change.

When I was sixteen going on seventeen, I was timid and afraid to venture into the unknown. I silently admired the way my brother handled his bicycle. Sometimes, he performed stunts in front of me to make me feel small. I used to hold on to the handlebars of the bicycle as I walked by it. I really wanted to ride the bicycle, but I did not have the guts to do it; I feared the unknown. Fear is false evidence appearing real.

We were a joint Hindu household, two families with sixteen family members under one roof. One Sunday morning, I was standing by the bicycle and admiring it. My uncle Kandasamy Chettiar, noticing this, told me to sit on the bicycle and pedal. He held on to the handlebars and rear of the seat to boost my confidence. He then let go of the handlebars and only held on to the rear of the seat. As my confidence level increased, after a few practice sessions, I ventured out on my own within my housing compound. A few more practice rides gave me the confidence to venture out into the streets near my house. This is my story of how I learned to ride the bicycle.

Now let us see how my story fits into the concept of conscious competence and the process of learning a new skill. This process has four stages.

1. When an individual does not know how to do something and is also unaware of the benefit of acquiring the skill, this is called *unconscious incompetence.* One will only change when one becomes aware of the value of the skill.
2. When an individual does not know how to do something but is aware of the benefit of acquiring the skill, this is called *conscious incompetence.* One will change when one acquires the knowledge.
3. When an individual knows how to do something and is aware of the benefit of acquiring the skill, this is called *conscious competence.* At this level, the individual has to concentrate and break down the skill into simple, achievable steps.
4. When an individual has mastered a skill, can perform it with ease, and can perform another task simultaneously, this is called *unconscious competence.* For example, a child struggles to tie his or her shoelaces the first time, but over time, the child masters the skill and is hardly conscious of it. Or when you pass your driving test and take the car on the road, you are very conscious every time you change gears. Over time,

it becomes second nature, and you multitask as you change gears. You have mastered the skill.

Learning to ride a bicycle is based on this process. A person who does not have the skill and does not appreciate the benefit of acquiring the skill will remain unconsciously incompetent. The minute he or she realizes the benefit of acquiring the skill but does not possess the skill, he or she becomes consciously incompetent, as I was. Then, when I acquired the skill with my uncle's help, I became consciously competent. Finally, when I mastered the skill, I became unconsciously competent. At this stage, I was able to do other things while riding the bicycle.

Most skills you acquire are based on this concept. You move up the ladder as you realize the importance of acquiring new skills. Your life changes based on your decisions. Master new skills, and enjoy the bounty life provides to you. Self-awareness is a trait for success.

When I was managing a fairly large grocery mini-market with a wet market, we managed the outlet as a family with about six staffs. Business was brisk; it kept my wife and me pretty busy. We were earning a decent living. I was living life consciously incompetent in the area of goal setting till I read a newspaper advert in 1990, which said, 'Earn a five-figure income. Attend our free preview.' I thought, *Why not attend the preview? I am only earning a four-figure income.* I garnered enough courage to make an appointment to attend the preview in Singapore, 120 kilometres from my town. When I attended the preview, I acquired knowledge on goal setting and the need to get a set of tools to start the process. I invested in a set of Success Motivational International (SMI) tools comprised of a manual, a workbook, and tapes. I started my goal-setting journey and became consciously competent in goal setting. Every day, I listened to the tapes in my car and used the manual and workbook diligently. It paved the way for me to change my life. The founder of SMI, Paul

J. Meyer, has said, 'Whatever you vividly imagine, ardently desire, sincerely believe and enthusiastically act upon must inevitably come to pass.'

All Dream Walkers have clearly defined goals. We have many options and distractions competing for our time, resources, and attention. We have too many things to do with the time and resources we have available. Dream Walkers focus only on activities that can lead them closer to their desired goals.

Let me share a mythological story I heard many years ago. There was a king who enjoyed hunting. On a fine, clear evening, the king set out into the woods with his men. He heard wriggling sounds coming from bushes and the mincing steps of a deer. A doe emerged shaking her coat, head, and eyelashes to clear the dust. The doe stiffened her legs and wriggled nervously into some bush pursued by the king with bow in hand. He took aim and shot, and the arrow grazed the prey, which moved swiftly, and pierced an earth mound. The mound burst open, and a sage emerged with furious, bloodshot eyes, cursing the king to life as a swine. The king pleaded for mercy, recollecting the incident. The sage said he would not be able to retract the curse, but if the crown prince, the heir to the throne, touched the king after a year, it would break the curse. The king sent the men back to the castle with the message, and he turned into a swine.

Time passed swiftly. On the anniversary of the curse, the prince returned to the woods with all the pomp and splendour the return of the king deserved. The prince searched and found the king boar amid a drove of pigs. The prince proclaimed to the king boar that he had come to break the curse and take him back to the palace. The huge king boar, with a big head and long snout, said, 'In the last year, I have found a sow, and she has bore me many piglets. I am very happy and contented. Now you go back and rule the country.'

Change is never easy. You fight to hold on. You fight
to let go.

—Daniel Stern

You could say it is only a mythological story. But the truth is many
people live this fantasy as truth day in and day out. They are not
willing to break away from the comfort zone and live their dream
lives. Familiarity breeds contentment. They accept a substandard
and mediocre life as their fated reality, without realizing their great
potential lying untapped. They will only change if they realize that
they have great, untapped potential or if an incident jolts them out of
their comfort zone. Dream Walkers believe in the great potential lying
untapped within them, and they diligently work towards realizing their
great potential. You, too, can be part of this team if you do what these
ordinary people do to get extraordinary results. You can awaken your
dream and walk towards it on your own; you don't have to wait for
something to jolt you awake or leave a tombstone with an untold story.

Again, in this chapter, I have captured my key thoughts as power
thoughts. If you have not completed the thirty days' reading of the
last two chapters, please combine the power thoughts, and read them
three times daily for the next thirty days to form new good habits.
The first reading should happen when you rise in the morning. Read
them again in the afternoon after lunch. Finally, read them aloud at
night just before you go to bed. The messages will become part of
your conscious mind. Then they will seep into your mysterious and
powerful subconscious mind, which creates your dreams. When you
keep repeating them joyfully with love, they will give birth to a new
habit you create consciously.

POWER THOUGHTS 3

Today, I affirm age has no bearing on success. I understand at any
age, I can achieve my dreams. I will never let others talk me into

abandoning my dreams by saying I am too young or too old. I enjoy my life the way I want to enjoy it.

I am aware life is all about choices. I understand my destiny unfolds according to my choices.

I am aware I need to follow my heart instead of the world. I understand all inventions, all progress, all advancements, and all discoveries came about because somebody had the courage not to listen to the crowd. I will get to the end of my life living my dreams. I am a Dream Walker with a vision and mission.

I am aware I have to set goals to put me on the mountaintop. I know the rewards will be fantastic. I know I will tap my unlimited potential, which has lain hidden and underutilized. I can feel the loving, caring, vibrant, and positive person I am transforming into in moving towards my goals.

I am aware time is a valuable and prized possession of mine. I am committed to managing my time efficiently. I love my time. I invest my time in activities that give me the desired results. I do not worry about the time I have squandered in the past. I know I can start fresh, valuing time from this very minute with vigour and belief. I am aware I need to master new skills and enjoy the bounty life provides.

CHAPTER 4

The Greatest Soul

My life is my message.

—Gandhi

Gandhi, also called 'Mahatma the Great Soul', was an advocate of nonviolence and a beacon of hope for oppressed and marginalized people. He inspired and influenced four Nobel Peace Prize laureates to use civil disobedience as the tool to achieve their objectives.

One of them was the first black president of South Africa, Nelson Mandela, who spent twenty-seven years of his life in prison fighting for equal rights for his people. Mandela, when unveiling the statue of Gandhi at the Gandhi Memorial, said, 'Gandhiji influenced the activities of liberation movements, civil rights movements and religious organizations in all five continents of the world. He had a huge impact on many men and women who have achieved significant historical changes in their countries.' This Nobel laureate said, 'Do not judge me by my successes, judge me by how many times I fell down and got back up again.'

The second Nobel Peace Prize laureate Gandhi influenced was Aung San Suu Kyi. She initiated a nonviolent movement towards achieving democracy and gaining human rights. She spent fifteen years under house arrest after her return to Myanmar in 1988. She said, 'Gandhi is somebody really phenomenal. I think you must all read his works, the more you read Gandhi, the more impressed you are by who he was and what he was.' She went on to say, 'You must remember that change through nonviolent means was not ever thought of before Gandhi. He was the one who started it, he was the one who decided that it is possible to bring about revolutionary change without violence.' This Iron Lady of Burma said, 'The only real prison is fear and the only real freedom is freedom from fear.'

The third Nobel Peace Prize laureate Gandhi influenced was Martin Luther King Jr., an American Baptist minister and leader of the African American civil rights movement who fought for equality. The activist and humanitarian best known for his role in the advancement of civil rights using civil disobedience was inspired by Gandhi's successful nonviolent movement. He took a trip to India that deepened his understanding of nonviolent resistance and his commitment to the African American struggle for civil rights. Sharing his reflection on the radio, he said, 'Since being in India, I am more convinced than ever before that the method of nonviolent resistance is the most potent weapon available to oppressed people in their struggle for justice and human dignity.' He shared with the world, 'Faith is taking the first step even when you don't see the staircase.'

The fourteenth Dalai Lama, Tenzin Gyatso, the fourth Nobel Peace Prize laureate and a great admirer of Gandhi, shared,

> I have the greatest respect for this great human being with deep understanding of human nature. He made every effort to encourage the full development of the positive aspects of the human potential and to reduce or restrain the negative. His life has inspired me ever since I was a small boy. Ahimsa or nonviolence is the powerful idea that Gandhi made familiar throughout the world. But nonviolence does not mean the mere

absence of violence. It is something more positive, more meaningful than that, for it depends wholly on the power of truth. The true expression of nonviolence is compassion.

Since the brutal suppression of the Tibetan Uprising by Chinese troops in 1959, the Dalai Lama has lived in exile in Dharamsala, India. The 1989 Nobel Peace Prize recipient for his nonviolent struggle for the liberation of Tibet shared his thoughts on happiness: 'Happiness is not something readymade. It comes from your own action.'

Mahatma the Great Soul, who was instrumental in instilling the spirit of nonviolence in these nonviolent laureates, also influenced millions of people globally. In his own gentle way, he shook the world.

Gandhi – born in Gujarat, India, on 2 October 1869 – was a mediocre student. On completion of his studies at the University of Bombay, he pursued the philosophical study of religions at the University College of London. He returned to India after being admitted to the English bar but found it difficult to get work. In 1893, he accepted a year's contract to work for an Indian legal firm in Natal, South Africa, but ended up spending twenty-one years there. During these years, he rallied against the injustice of discrimination, and on one occasion, he was thrown from a first-class train carriage, despite being in possession of a valid ticket.

On his return to India In 1916, Gandhi developed his practice of nonviolent civil disobedience. He encouraged oppressed villagers to improve their own circumstances while leading peaceful strikes and protests. By 1921, Gandhi led the Indian National Congress and reorganized the party's constitution on *Swaraj* principle, which is complete political independence from the British. He instigated a boycott of British goods and institutions. His encouragement of mass civil disobedience led to his arrest in 1922 and trial on sedition charges. He was sentenced to a six-year prison term, but he served only two years. In 1930, he led a famous 250-mile march to the sea to collect his own salt when the British introduced a tax on salt.

Recognizing Gandhi's political influence, the British authorities were forced to negotiate various settlements over the years that followed. This resulted in alleviating poverty, granting status to the 'untouchables', and enshrining rights for women. This finally led to Gandhi's goal of *Swaraj*, political independence from Britain in 1947. Gandhi, always dressed in a woven loincloth, led a modest life. He shared, 'In a gentle way, you can shake the world.' That is what he did.

Let us look at his philosophical thoughts on life.

> Keep your thoughts positive because your thoughts become your words. Keep your words positive because your words become your behaviour. Keep your behaviour positive because your behaviour becomes your habits. Keep your habits positive because your habits become your values. Keep your values positive because your values become your destiny.
>
> —Gandhi

Positive thoughts are the starting point to move towards your destiny. It is a process of evolution towards your destiny which could be simultaneous or one after another. ... Success is inevitable if you remain positive at all times believing that you will reach your destiny. Belief in yourself will ultimately lead you towards your dream and goal. Change yourself – you are in control.

If you want to be in control of your life, it must start with you. When you change your thinking, your feelings will change, and this will, in turn, lead to new actions. You will realize the world around you is also changing, since you are viewing the environment with new lenses.

When you are in control of your life, you can choose the thoughts, reactions, and emotions you want to accept. You don't have to freak out, overreact, or even react in a negative way. You can choose to act positively on the information you receive because you are in control.

When you are in control, you take total responsibility for all the thoughts running through your brain. There is no place for any negative thoughts. You are the father of every thought originating from you. All outcomes originate from your thinking, which moves you to your behaviour, and the final product, which is the outcome.

When you are in control, the old thought patterns of guilt, anger, unhappiness, and blame will be replaced by new, empowering thought patterns of happiness, appreciation, cooperation, understanding, and love. Gandhi said, 'A coward is incapable of exhibiting love; it is the prerogative of the brave.' When you are in control, you will feel as Gandhi said: 'Nobody can hurt me without my permission.' How you feel, how you respond, and how you react to a given situation are entirely up to you. You are in the driver's seat; you are in control.

Let me share with you the story of Viktor Frankl, an Austrian neurologist and psychiatrist who was deported to a Nazi prison camp in 1942 with his wife and parents. There, he worked as a general practitioner. Then in 1944, he and his wife were transferred to a camp where he worked as a slave labourer. In the Holocaust, he lost his mother, brother, and wife. His sister, the only survivor among his immediate family members, migrated to Australia. Frankl once said, 'Everything can be taken from a man but one thing: the last of human freedoms – to choose one's attitude in any given set of circumstances, to choose one's own way.'

Thoughts are very potent. Whatever thoughts you harbour and give energy to manifest themselves today. Whatever thoughts you hold today and give energy to will manifest tomorrow. We are all the product of our thoughts.

A man is but a product of his thoughts. What he thinks, he becomes.

—Gandhi

If painful memories cause you suffering and paralyse you from taking action, you must learn to forgive, forget, and let go to live your dreams as you were born to live. Gandhi said, 'The weak can never forgive. Forgiveness is an attribute of the strong.' You decide if you are weak or strong. You decide if you are in control or if others are in control. Just think of what Viktor Frankl said before making your decision.

Without action, you aren't going anywhere.

—Gandhi

To achieve anything, you need to take action. Taking action can be difficult, and the resistance from within can be overwhelming. It is easy to talk about taking action, but to put it into action can be quite a task. When you are in control of your life, you will move swiftly to take action. If necessary, you will take massive action.

Gandhi said, 'I will not let anyone walk through my mind with their dirty feet.' When you think of these great words by Gandhi, you should get charged. Never let people walk through your mind with dirty feet. They have no right to steal a moment, an hour, or a day from you. They have no right to make you feel miserable and unhappy. Just shield yourself and say, 'I am in control. Nobody can hurt me without my permission.' Repeat this till you take complete control and command of the situation.

Glory lies in the attempt to reach one's goal and not
in reaching it.

—Gandhi

The minute an idea, a dream, or a goal is born, you have to nurture
and care for it in order for it to grow and bear fruit. You will definitely
achieve the results if the nurturing is done well. If you have planted
a mango seed, you will have a mango tree bearing mango fruits. You
can't expect papayas from a mango tree. You have to plant papaya
seeds if you want papayas. So the same applies to your dreams; you
can't keep changing your dreams and expect better results. If you
sow a thought, you have to nurture it and care for it till it gives the
desired results. So focus and glorify the process, and you will inevitably
achieve the end result.

Please bear in mind about sixty thousand thoughts cross your mind
daily. You will never hit a target if you do not have focus. It is ideal if
you can put your goals in writing and read them daily. It is excellent to
commit your goals to paper; this affects your awareness. Your awareness
will shape your choices, and your choices will shape your results. Your
goals can be short term, to achieve within six months, twelve months,
or eighteen months; or medium term, to achieve within two years,
three years, or four years; or long term, to achieve within five years, ten
years, or longer. If it is a complex goal, you should probably maintain
a separate journal to monitor your progress. Once you decide on your
goal, work towards its achievement with total commitment. Keep in
mind what Tony Robbins has said: 'It is in your moments of decision
your destiny is shaped.'

When you make a promise and honour it, or when you work towards
a goal you have set, you control your life immediately. Even small
commitments and successes give you courage and strength to accept
greater responsibilities. Your belief system grows as you keep progressing.
You have control over your knowledge, skills, and desires. You can work

towards improving them and making them effective. Have a well-thought-out plan of action that takes into consideration your strengths, weaknesses, opportunities, and threads. Your plan of action should be flexible to capitalize on it or correct it where and when necessary.

> When it is obvious that the goal cannot be reached,
> don't adjust the goal, adjust the action steps.
>
> —Confucius

The great teacher Confucius highlighted the importance of being focused on the steps. When you meet an obstacle, don't just adjust or abandon the goal; ensure you have followed the steps diligently. It is vital to relook at the action plan and ensure you have followed the steps. If necessary, start the action all over again.

Another thinker is Thiruvalluvar, who wrote *Thirukkural*, a collection of 1,330 rhyming Tamil *kural* (couplets or aphorisms), more than two thousand years ago. This work of Thiruvalluvar is considered one of the most important works in Tamil literature, covering almost all aspects of life. I share with you kural 596: 'Let your thoughts be high and lofty always. You may fail but your zeal stays.' Think of rising higher. Let it be your only thought. Even if you don't attain the object, the thought itself will raise you.

Great men think alike. The great Gandhi says the glory lies in the attempt to reach one's goal. He means that you should rejoice in the process of moving towards your goal. If you undertake the process with joy, dedication, and belief, you will inevitably achieve your goal. The great Confucius says you should never abandon your goals just because you are facing obstacles. He says you should reevaluate your steps and embark on new actions where necessary, whereas Thiruvalluvar says unwavering thoughts will lead you to great success. Even if you fall short of achieving the desired result, you will still be elevated to a higher thought level.

The power-packed Bruce Lee said, 'A goal is not always meant to be reached. It often serves simply as something to aim at.'

Your actions will be a reflection of your thoughts and words. If your thoughts, words, and deeds are congruent, you will enjoy happiness and inner joy.

> Happiness is when what you think, what you say, and what you do are in harmony.
>
> —Gandhi

Your communication through your voice, tone, and body language will show whether your words and thoughts are positively aligned or negatively aligned.

> Be congruent, be authentic, be your true self.
>
> —Gandhi

The language you use will reflect your response or reaction to a situation. When you *respond*, you act positively, and when you *react*, you act negatively. Your words are your thoughts made verbal, and they broadcast your belief. Your results are the final product of your belief driving you to your behaviour.

> Live as if you were to die tomorrow. Learn as if you were to live forever.
>
> —Gandhi

Death is a reality, but most of us are not ready for it. It is a fact. Let's say tomorrow is your last day; what would you do first? List all the things you want to accomplish. Be sincere and genuine. Start every day with the end in mind. You will definitely look forward to every minute. Life will definitely get better and be fruitful. You will cherish every moment as precious and love it.

The habit of reading is a must for success. Reading is a habit everyone aspiring for success in life needs to do. Be selective in what you read. You must read something that can take you to the next phase of your life. It could relate to your career, your hobbies, your faith, or your dreams. You should spend at least thirty to sixty minutes a day reading in areas that matter most to you. Definitely, something positive will happen in your life. Walt Disney said, 'There is more treasure in books than in all the pirates' loot on Treasure Island and best of all, you can enjoy these riches every day of your life.'

It is scientifically proven that reading can increase your intelligence, boost your brainpower, make you smarter, make you empathetic, help fight Alzheimer's disease, and help you relax and sleep better if you read before bedtime. A report suggests that if you read out loud to a six- to ten-year-old kid, it will most likely inspire the kid to develop the habit of reading five to seven times a week for fun.

You need knowledge to realize your dreams. You can acquire knowledge by reading, listening, seeing, touching, tasting, or smelling, or using all your senses. Knowledge must be applied to be manifested. Knowledge is only potential power until you take daily action. Take action – massive action to benefit from the power of knowledge.

> First they ignore you, then they laugh at you, then they fight you, then you win.
>
> —Gandhi

Be persistent; don't give up. The time taken to achieve something need not work out as you plan. If you believe in yourself, act enthusiastic, develop your skills, and take action, it will come to pass. Do not let your inner resistance weaken your willpower. When you stand out and drive yourself towards better results, you could face obstacles. This could lead to self-doubt. Success is inevitable if your faith and belief in yourself are unfaltering.

> No matter how insignificant the thing you have to
> do, do it as well as you can, give it as much of your
> care and attention as you would give to the thing you
> regard as most important. For it will be by those small
> things that you shall be judged.
>
> —Gandhi

You must learn to treat everything you do as important. Even the insignificant things you do are important. If the janitor who cleans the toilet considers his job insignificant, then we will have a hard time using the toilet. As Martin Luther King Jr. said, 'If a man is called to be a street sweeper, he should sweep streets even as a Michelangelo painted, or Beethoven composed music or Shakespeare wrote poetry. He should sweep streets so well that all the hosts of heaven and earth will pause to say, "Here lived a great street sweeper who did his job well."'

The insignificant becomes significant when you do it with pride and passion. When you assign importance to every small detail, then everything becomes important and significant. You will give your best to every assignment you undertake. You start feeling good and performing better. One reason Gandhi was so successful with his method of nonviolence was because he and his followers were so persistent and passionate. They just didn't give up. Before Gandhi, the world thought success could only be attained through violence or aggression. He changed the world to accept there is an option called *nonviolence*.

Dream Walkers believe in love, understanding, and appreciation. Dream Walkers seek to understand others first. Dream Walkers listen to the other side of an argument and do not prejudge. They love and appreciate others unconditionally. They believe in *you win* and *I win*.

POWER THOUGHTS 4

Today, I realize I have to keep my thoughts positive, as they become my words. I realize I have to keep my words positive, as they become my behaviour. I realize I have to keep my behaviour positive, as it becomes my habits. I realize I have to keep my habits positive, as they become my values. I realize I have to keep my values positive, as they become my destiny.

Today, I realize I am in control of my life. I realize when I change my thinking, my feelings change, and this leads to new actions. I choose the thoughts, reactions, and emotions I want to accept because I am in control. I realize the world around me is also changing, since I am viewing the environment through new lenses.

Today, I have decided to remove feelings of guilt, anger, and unhappiness from my mind and replace them with empowering thoughts of happiness, appreciation, cooperation, love, and understanding. I have forgiven all those people against whom I harboured vengeance, hatred, and unhappiness.

Today, I am a new person, making it my priority to take action to achieve my dreams and goals. I do not procrastinate. I am in control; nobody can hurt me without my permission.

Today, I have decided to spend thirty to sixty minutes a day reading about subjects that will move me towards achieving my dreams and goals.

CHAPTER 5

I Am the Greatest

The greatest jihad or the greatest war is the war over
oneself.

—Prophet Mohammed

The loud-talking, flamboyant, strong-willed Muhammad Ali was born
Cassius Marcellus Clay Jr. in the United States in 1942. Considered
one of the greatest boxers in history, he won both the coveted Golden
Gloves title and an Olympic gold medal. He grew up in the segregated
South, experiencing racial prejudice and discrimination firsthand,
which likely contributed to his early passion for boxing.

Returning to the ring in 1970, Ali had another legendary fight
that took place in 1974. Billed the *Rumble in the Jungle*, it was held
in Kinshasa, Zaire, Africa. Ali fought the reigning heavyweight
champion, George Foreman. For once, Ali was seen as the underdog
to his younger and powerful opponent. In the fight, Ali used his
rope-a-dope strategy. The Oxford dictionary explains Muhammad Ali
coined the term *rope-a-dope* in 1974, referring to a tactic in a boxing
match with George Foreman. The boxing tactic involved pretending
to be trapped against the ropes and goading an opponent to throw
tiring, ineffective punches; Ali utilized this strategy to shock George
Foreman.

I could feel the fight's enthusiasm and excitement even after forty years when I watched the fight recently on YouTube with live commentary by Jim Brown, Joe Frazier, David Frost, and Bob Sheridan. Widespread publicity and news flashes by the world's media created great expectations for the fight, which pitted an undefeated, overwhelming-favourite world champion against a well-worn, thirty-two-year-old former world champion in a stadium packed with sixty thousand spectators.

I am excited to share with you excerpts from an old interview with Ali in *Playboy* magazine. In it, 'the Greatest' explains in detail why he opted to suddenly change course after the first round versus Foreman in an unorthodox and risky rope-a-dope plan, which had never been used in the history of the sport: 'Well, I didn't really plan it. After the first round, I felt myself getting too tired for the pace of that fight, but George wasn't gonna get tired, 'cause he was just cutting the ring off on me,' states Ali. 'I stayed out of the way but I figured that after seven or eight rounds of dancing like that, I'd be really tired. Then, when I'd go to the ropes, my resistance would be low and George would get one through to me. So while I was still fresh, I decided to go on the ropes and try to get George tired.'

Ali, aged thirty-two, reveals his original game plan to combat the undefeated twenty-four-year-old Foreman was a mistake: 'I had it in mind to do what I did when I was 22, "to dance every round," but I got tired so I had to change my strategy. George didn't change his strategy, 'cause he can't do nothin' but attack – that's the only thing he knows. All he wants to do is get his man in the corner, so in the second round I gave him what he wanted. He couldn't do nothin'.'

Ali says Foreman couldn't land any decisive hits in the second round, but he kept trying and trying: 'He just figured he'd get me in the next round. When he didn't do it in the third, he thought he'd get me in the fourth. Then he thought it would be in the fifth, and then in the sixth. But in the sixth round George was so tired. All of a sudden he knew he'd thrown everything he had at me and hadn't hurt me at all. And he just lost all his heart.'

Ali says he was able to sense Foreman losing his self-belief by the way his determination withered: 'He stopped attacking the way he'd been doing. He had shots to take and he didn't take them. And then I purposefully left him some openings and he wouldn't take them. George knew he'd been caught in my trap and there wasn't but one way he could get out of it – by knocking me out. He kept trying with his last hope but he was too tired and a man of his age and talent shouldn't get used up that quick. George was dead tired. He was throwing wild punches, missing and falling over the ropes.'

Foreman underestimated him in several ways; Ali concludes, 'He didn't realize how hard I am to hit and how hard I can hit. He thought he was greater than me. Well, George is humble now. I did just what I told him I'd do when the ref was giving us instructions. There was George trying to scare me with his serious look – he got that from his idol Sonny Liston. And there I was *telling him*, "Boy, you're in trouble. You're gonna meet the greatest fighter of all time. We here now and there ain't no way for you to get out of this ring – I gotcha! You been readin' about me since you were a little boy and now you gonna see me in action. Chump, I'm gonna show you how great I am. I'm gonna eat you up! You don't stand a chance! You lose the crown tonight!"'

Muhammad Ali knocked out George Foreman in the eighth round with a flurry of punches, in one of the most sensational moments in sports history. Success is about employing the right game plan at the right time. After the first round, Ali realized that his original game plan was not going to work against the young George Foreman. Ali decided his quote 'Float like a butterfly and sting like a bee' wasn't going to work. So he decided to go on the rope to get George tired. His game plan worked, and he knocked George out in the eighth round to regain the world title and prove his tactical genius. This is a great lesson for all of us. We, too, have to be like Ali, changing our game plan when the situation warrants it. We can't employ an old game plan we think will not work or one that is not working.

You can learn inspiring lessons from Ali, one of the greatest athletes in boxing history. Let me share with you some of his powerful sayings that apply to the traits of Dream Walkers.

TRAIT 1: POSITIVE WORDS HAVE POWER

Dream Walkers always speak with the end in mind. They believe using positive vocabulary will germinate into reality. Words are very potent. Select the right words to describe you. Ali always thought and said, 'I am the greatest.' This positive vibration created his reality. What words do you use? Are you using the right vocabulary to create your reality? What words will you use to create your reality?

As I said in the first chapter, when a thought is repeated over and over, it becomes your belief and your truth. Your belief determines your behaviour. When you say something is possible or not possible, you are personally right. If you want new results, just change your thought, and keep repeating it to form your new belief and your new truth.

> I am the greatest. I said that even before I knew I was.
> —Muhammad Ali

TRAIT 2: VISUALIZATION IS POWER

Deep inside you, there lies a Dream Walker, a champion, and a visionary with desires and goals. If you can visualize the unseen with deep feeling and emotions, it will become your reality. If you can do this three times a day, the results can be astonishing.

Every single creation in this world had its origin in someone's mind in picture form. This picture was perfected through the imaginative process. To get outstanding results, just envision a perfect result of your goals in your mind.

> Champions aren't made in the gyms. Champions are made from something they have deep inside them – a desire, a dream, a vision.
>
> —Muhammad Ali

TRAIT 3: ACTIONS SPEAK LOUDER THAN WORDS

It is said actions speak louder than words. The intensity of your actions will decide the level of your success. Habitually, once Dream Walkers make a decision, they take immediate action and do not procrastinate. You may not enjoy the actions you take. But all winners take action – if necessary, massive action – with the end in mind.

To enjoy the fruits of a desired result, you need to focus and live your life with the end in mind. Start thinking what actions by you today will give you your desired end results. Let the results be the legacy you wish to leave behind or the way you want to be remembered.

Successful people are disciplined. By being self-disciplined, we are willing to postpone gratification till we achieve our dreams. I might not like doing something, but I just do it, as it needs to be done to achieve my goal. It is best for me to be tough on myself now so that life will be easier on me later. I could start the day thirty minutes earlier to enjoy quality time by myself. There are so many choices like this I can make daily. The decisions I make from the choices I have will shape the quality of my life.

I hated every minute of training, but I said, 'Don't quit. Suffer now and live the rest of your life as a champion.'

—Muhammad Ali

TRAIT 4: HAVE FAITH AND BELIEVE

Dream Walkers believe they were born to live their dreams and be achievers. Their faith in their belief system transforms the ordinary vibrations of their thoughts to their spiritual equivalent.

It's lack of faith that makes people afraid of meeting challenges, and I believed in myself.

—Muhammad Ali

TRAIT 5: SUCCESS IS A MIND GAME

Dream Walkers believe in victory before they enjoy the fruits in reality. Their minds are tuned to believe they can achieve. Through affirmation and visualization, you must accept that you must flood your mind with victorious thoughts at all times, as success is a mind game.

The fight is won or lost far away from witnesses – behind the lines, in the gym, and out there on the road, long before I dance under those lights.

—Muhammad Ali

Muhammad Ali's approach to life made him a Dream Walker with faith, determination, guts, persistence, hard work, and a winning attitude.

It's hard to beat a guy when he's got his mind made up that he's going to win.

—Muhammad Ali

If your attitude to win is rock solid, then nothing can move you away from your goal. They say you see obstacles if you take your eyes off your goals. If you have a winning attitude every day, you will stay focused on your goals with powerful affirmations and visualizations.

TRAIT 6: AFFIRMATIONS HAVE POWER

It's the repetition of affirmations that leads to belief. And once that belief becomes a deep conviction, things begin to happen.

—Muhammad Ali

This is a very powerful trait you need to master to create a winning attitude. You must convince yourself that you have faith in whatever you are asking for. Things will only start happening when you have deep conviction. Affirmations are deliberately repeated thoughts about yourself that you have decided to make come true.

Research has proven a new thought pattern taking root and growing will require repeating the affirmation at least five to ten times daily. You could prepare your affirmation on three sets of two-inch by four-inch cards, laminate them, and keep them in your room at home, your office, and your car, as, to get the best results, you should repeat it in the morning, at noon, and just before bedtime. The affirmation must be personal, feature *I*, be in the present tense, be positive, visual, and emotional. You must be able to see yourself as achieving and feeling the emotions. Don't get discouraged if you do not get the desired results you expect; keep at it. As Ali said, 'I am the greatest, I said that even before I knew I was.'

TRAIT 7: RISK TAKING HAS POWER

He who is not courageous enough to take risks will accomplish nothing in life.

—Muhammad Ali

Dream Walkers are risk takers. They are like eagles; you find them one at a time. Dream Walkers refuse to buy into what others say is impossible. You must be courageous to take risks if you want to enjoy the fruits of your labour. If you want to live a great life, you must be willing to take great risks. You should plan, take council from knowledgeable people, evaluate, and take calculated risks. You should follow your heart and take instructions from your conscience. Being knowledgeable is a sure way to avoid unwanted risk. Once you have decided, do not procrastinate. Just do it.

Ali kept his words, thoughts, and deeds in formation. His words were a true reflection of his thoughts, reflected in the final act. He lived true to every word of Gandhi: 'Happiness is when what you think, what you say, and what you do are in harmony.'

Dream Walkers are people who possess these seven traits. You must diligently work on these traits to join the club of Dream Walkers. They are ordinary people focused on achieving the extraordinary. Their faith and belief in themselves are etched into their flesh; nothing can deter them from achieving their goals. They utter positive words in the present tense, using *I* at all times. This prelude serves to create their reality. Dream Walkers know success is a mind game. You must flood your mind with powerful affirmations of the qualities you are focused on and visualize the end results as vividly as possible. Dream Walkers are risk takers taking action on a priority basis.

POWER THOUGHTS 5

I always speak with the end in mind. I believe in using positive words daily. I believe words are very powerful and potent. I select the right words to describe me.

I am a champion and visionary with desires and goals. I visualize the unseen with deep feeling and emotion; it is becoming my reality. I do these visualizations three times a day and enjoy the astonishing results.

In my mind, I envision the perfect results of my goals. Every single creation in this world originated in the minds of our forefathers in picture form. They perfected these pictures in their imaginations. I employ the same process to get my perfect results.

The intensity of my actions will decide the level of my success. Once I decide, I take action, and I do not procrastinate. I've learned to enjoy every action I take.

I believe I was born to live my dreams and be an achiever. This faith in my belief system transforms the ordinary vibrations of my thoughts to their spiritual equivalent.

I believe in victory even before I enjoy the fruits in reality. My mind is tuned to believe I can achieve. I flood my mind with victorious thoughts, affirmations, and visualizations at all times, as success is a mind game.

I have deep conviction, faith, and a winning attitude to achieve whatever I ask for. I have decided to make it come true.

I am a Dream Walker. I am a knowledgeable risk taker following my dreams.

CHAPTER 6

Habits

A man who conquers himself is greater than one who conquers a thousand men in battle.

—Gautama Buddha

The power-packed Bruce Lee was born in San Francisco in 1940 but moved to Hong Kong, where he became a child star. His first film was called *The Birth of Mankind*. As Bruce Lee was getting himself into fights, he decided to take up kung fu to discipline himself. Bruce picked up his basic skills from the famous Yip Man. He quickly mastered kung fu and then wing chun, a branch of the Chinese martial arts, before progressing to his own style of jeet kune do, absorbing the best of various martial arts and philosophies. His style revolved around a central theme – absorbing what was useful, discarding what was useless, and constantly adapting to the ever-changing environment. Training was divided into different ranges, such as punching, kicking, grappling, and trapping.

At the age of nineteen, Lee left Hong Kong to pursue a degree in philosophy at the University of Washington in America. He began to teach some of his skills to students who would pay. Lee faced many confrontations and duels to remain, as some of the Japanese schools in the Seattle area tried to force him out. His martial arts school flourished. He met his wife, Linda, while studying there. He gave regular displays at exhibitions, and it was during one of these exhibitions that a producer spotted him and signed him up to do the Green Hornet series, which was a huge hit in Hong Kong.

In Hong Kong, Raymond Chow, the head of Golden Harvest, got Lee to act in his production *The Big Boss*. In September 1971, the second of the contractual films, *Fist of Fury*, also called *The Chinese Connection*, commenced production. It was a bigger success than the first film, breaking all-time box-office records. Bruce Lee formed a partnership with Raymond Chow called Concord Production for his third film, *The Way of the Dragon*, also titled *Return of the Dragon*. Bruce Lee produced, wrote, and directed this movie. The next film was *Enter the Dragon*. Making this movie was a stressful time for Lee, as he wanted the film to be good and well accepted by Western audiences. *Enter the Dragon* was due to premier at Hollywood's Chinese Theatre in August 1973. Unfortunately, Lee would not live to see the opening of his film, nor would he experience the accumulated success of more than thirty years of all his films' popularity. On 20 July 1973, the world lost a brilliant star and an evolved human being that day, only thirty-two years old.

Let me share with you eleven powerful quotes from this great star, which all of us can use for our success.

HABIT 1: BE YOURSELF

It's about unleashing the best version of you. Always be yourself, express yourself, and have faith in yourself. Bruce Lee was a performance-based trainer. He felt anybody could make mistakes but people must be courageous and take ownership.

> Mistakes are always forgivable, if one has the courage to admit them.
> —Bruce Lee

When you make mistakes, you also learn in the process. Your learning should give you the wisdom to know when to avoid and how to avoid making the same mistakes in the future. The strong are courageous to admit their mistakes. The weak will not admit their mistakes but will blame others for them. You decide if you want to be strong or you want to be weak.

HABIT 2: KEEP AN OPEN MIND; ABSORB THE BEST

If your mind is like a glass full of water, then it will not absorb anything new. You must be willing to let go of the limiting beliefs you harbour. Create space for new thoughts by emptying your glass. Take the best of the best, and tailor it to your needs. Lee borrowed concepts and techniques from every art in a relentless pursuit of the best. Bruce Lee developed *jeet kune do* based on this concept.

> Absorb what is useful, discard what is not and add what is uniquely yours.
>
> —Bruce Lee

To get what you want in life, you must first be willing to unlearn and then relearn. Many of your old thoughts and actions might not fit into your new environment. They can be stumbling blocks for your progress in the new pursuit. Affirmations and visualizations are powerful tools you must use to guide you towards your new direction when you relearn.

Empowering new habits are the milestones that can prepare you for the opportunities waiting to greet you. You must be ready to discard your old bad habits, which act as stumbling blocks to your progress. You must nurture the new empowering habits, which will replace your old bad habits. Only a new habit can replace an old unwanted habit. You must convey the new habit to your conscious mind daily. For this to happen, read your power thoughts three times daily for the next thirty days to form these new habits. The first reading should happen when you rise in the morning; then the second time should occur in the afternoon after lunch. Finally, read them aloud at night just before you go to bed. The messages will become part of your conscious mind. Then they will seep into your mysterious and powerful subconscious mind, which creates your dreams. When you keep repeating them joyfully with love, they will give birth to a new habit. You create this new habit consciously.

HABIT 3: AIM BEYOND YOUR TARGET

Aim past your target, and push past your limits. If you fall short, you still land in the ballpark of success. In the same way, an athlete competing in the high-jump track event practises setting the bar one notch higher than his or her best. Bruce Lee was famous for his one-inch punch, but in reality, he aimed past the one inch.

> Don't fear failure. Not failure, but low aim, is the crime. In great attempts it is glorious even to fail.
>
> —Bruce Lee

To maintain passion and live the life of your choice, you must set challenging goals. Goals are moving targets that change with your ability to analyse and project growth. Many people set goals that are not challenging and are easy to achieve. On achieving a goal, they sit on their laurels and wait. Over time, complacency sets in, and they are going nowhere. They lose focus; they become unproductive, frustrated, and disappointed. On the other hand, if they have challenging goals, they will be excited, stay productive, and move forward in their life. They will look forward to every day with excitement. So choose challenging goals that will excite you, keep your adrenaline flowing, and bring the best out of you. You were born to live the life of your choice; have an exciting pursuit of your dreams through your goals.

HABIT 4: STAY FLEXIBLE

Be flexible in your approach. Learn from everybody and everything, and don't get locked into a particular style.

Expose yourself to various conditions and learn.

—Bruce Lee

You must keep an open mind to learn from anybody, under any situation, or from any book. Don't reject knowledge without giving it a fair chance to evaluate it. The knowledge you acquire has to be processed and evaluated before you decide to accept or reject it. Once you have accepted it, use the learning effectively for your success. Please understand knowledge by itself is not power, but when you apply the knowledge, it is powerful.

HABIT 5: MASTER YOUR MIND AND BODY

You must be smart to understand that you need to work on your body and mind simultaneously to succeed. It's not sufficient to just master your body or your mind. Your body and mind must support each other. Your body helps turn what you think or dream into results.

As you think, so shall you become.

—Bruce Lee

Your body is a building block for your success. Many people neglect this basic principle and focus on all others. Your body needs to be exercised, nurtured, and cared for to get the desired results. The right food of the right quality and the right quantity gives the right nutrients. The right exercise tones your muscles and keeps you fit. The right breathing techniques carry enough oxygen to every organ, cell, and tissue. When your body is in excellent condition, in combination with the seven strategies discussed in the previous chapter, you shall become as you think.

A 1998 Harvard study concluded that a brisk thirty-minute walk five days a week reduces the risk of stroke by 24 per cent. It can also add seven hours to your life a week, which can be translated into fifteen days a year. Wouldn't it be great to add a bonus seven hours a week and fifteen days a year to your life? You choose if you spend your life in health or illness.

A number of studies carried out over the last ten years have concluded that physical activities reduce the risk of heart disease, diabetes, colon cancer, and breast cancer. The same physical activities improve cognitive functioning and resistance to disease and decrease the likelihood of entering a nursing home.

HABIT 6: APPLY WHAT YOU KNOW

Life is not about watching from the sidelines. Use what you know, and put knowledge into practice. Test yourself.

> Knowing is not enough; we must do. Willing is not
> enough; we must apply.
> —Bruce Lee

You can't achieve your goals just by saying, 'I know, and I am willing.' You must get into action by applying what you know. Actions speak louder than words. Actions will move you towards your goals. Every day, you must plan some activities towards realizing your goals. Even small steps taken on a daily basis will move you towards your goals.

> The truth of the matter is that you always know the
> right thing to do. The hard part is doing it.
> —Norman Schwarzkopf

HABIT 7: MAKE THINGS HAPPEN

When there is no wave, make one.

To hell with circumstances; I create opportunities.

—Bruce Lee

It really boils down to making the most of what you've got, including your mind and body; pushing past your limits; and following a path of continuous learning and growth. You proactively create the circumstances to meet with opportunities. This will lead you to the success you are pursuing.

HABIT 8: LIVE

You are a spiritual being in a physical body. Life is like a boomerang; anything you give will come back to you in a bountiful amount. Universal forces will reward you bountifully when you give with an open heart. If you give love, you receive bountiful love. If you give appreciation, you receive bountiful appreciation. If you give money, you receive bountiful money. If you believe you are endowed with something, that thing will flow into your life. Everything starts with your belief.

The game of life is a game of boomerangs. Our thoughts, deeds and words return to us sooner or later with astounding accuracy.

—Florence Scovel Shinn

Be cautious; if you transmit negative thoughts, you will receive bountiful amounts of negativity. If you give hatred, you receive bountiful hatred. If you are miserable, misery will flow into your life. Life starts with your beliefs, whether they be good or bad.

Real living is living for others.

—Bruce Lee

HABIT 9: BE AWARE

Many live unaware of the great potential bottled up inside them to be released. Knowledge is the genie waiting for your command to serve. When you reach a state of great awareness, the genie will appear. Your wish is its command.

First, you acquire knowledge; then, you apply the knowledge with the awareness you acquired. Some people, even with knowledge, are sceptical. I have shared many success stories in this book for the benefit of sceptics. You decide if you will walk in darkness or light!

Those who are unaware they are walking in darkness
will never seek the light.

—Bruce Lee

HABIT 10: AVOID NEGATIVE THOUGHTS

Even a single negative thought is cancerous. Nip it in the bud; never let it bloom. If you energize your negative thoughts or worries, the consequences can be disastrous. Convert all negative thoughts to positive thoughts. Shield yourself from negative thoughts, and let positive thoughts energize you by constantly chanting positive slogans. As Muhammad Ali said, 'It's the repetition of affirmations that leads to belief. And once that belief becomes a deep conviction, things begin to happen.'

Never waste energy on worries or negative thoughts,
all problems are brought into existence – drop them.

—Bruce Lee

HABIT 11: DON'T ACCEPT DEFEAT

You are never defeated until you accept defeat. If you do not get the desired results, it does not mean you have failed. It tells you that you have not done something right to get the desired results. It merely means you have to reevaluate and adjust to get the desired results.

You may have faced many adversities. You may feel the share of defeats you have faced is far more than your fair share. Instead of worrying, you should accept the unfavourable results as lessons to enrich your life and prepare you for the greater opportunities waiting for you.

> Defeat is a state of mind; no one is ever defeated until defeat has been accepted as a reality.
> —Bruce Lee

Oprah Winfrey says, 'There is no such thing as failure; failure is just life trying to move us in another direction.'

Every Dream Walker is a success in his or her own way with a story to share with the world. You, too, can be a Dream Walker with a success story to share. What are you doing to create your success story? Are you willing to travel the extra mile to live your dreams? Are you willing to invest in yourself to create your success story? Are you willing to pursue your dreams relentlessly with passion, perseverance, and perspective? If you are, then you must start at this very moment. As Lao Tzu said, 'A journey of thousand miles begins with the first step.'

POWER THOUGHTS 6

Today, I unleash the best version of me. I always express myself and have faith in myself. I am a strong and courageous person, ready to accept my mistakes. I realize making mistakes is a learning process that gives me the wisdom to know when to avoid and how to avoid making the same mistakes and to enjoy the journey.

I do not harbour limiting beliefs. I create space for new thoughts. I take the best thoughts and tailor them to my needs. I am willing to unlearn and relearn. I am willing to discard thoughts that don't fit into my new environment. I use affirmations and visualizations to guide me towards my new thoughts. I aim past my target and push past my limits.

I empower myself with new habits that prepare me for the opportunities waiting for me. I discard old bad habits, which are the stumbling blocks for my progress. I realize a new habit must replace an old unwanted habit. To convey the new habit to my conscious mind, I read affirmations to form these new habits three times daily for thirty days. I do the first reading when I rise in the morning; then, the second reading is in the afternoon after lunch; and the final reading happens aloud at night just before I go to bed. These messages then will seep into my mysterious and powerful subconscious mind, which creates my dreams. When I keep repeating them joyfully with love, they will give birth to a new habit.

I set challenging goals, which are exciting and productive. My goals are moving targets that change with my ability to analyse and project growth. I look forward to every day with excitement. I was born to live the life of my choice.

I am flexible in my approach to life. I learn from everybody and everything. I keep an open mind to learn from anybody, under any situation, or from any book. I process and evaluate the knowledge I have acquired before I decide to accept or reject it. Once I have accepted it, I use the learning effectively for my success. I realize knowledge is only power when I apply it. Applied knowledge is power.

I am aware my body is a building block for my success. I exercise regularly to tone my muscles and keep fit. I consume quality food that gives my body the right nutrients. I've learned the right breathing techniques to carry enough oxygen to my every organ, cell, and tissue. I love my body. I care for my body. My body is in excellent condition.

I know actions speak louder than words and will move me towards my goal. Every day, I plan activities towards realizing my goals. I realize even small steps taken on a daily basis will move me towards my goal.

I push past my limits in following the path of continuous learning and growth. I proactively create circumstances that meet me with opportunities to achieve success.

I am a spiritual being in a physical body. The universal forces reward me bountifully when I give with an open heart. I believe I am endowed and everything positive is flowing into me.

I only accept positive thoughts. Any negative thought, I nip it in the bud. I shield myself from negative thoughts by constantly chanting positive slogans.

I am a Dream Walker with a success story to share with the world.

CHAPTER 7

An Extraordinary Life

Work is not your enemy but your friend. How you work, not what you do, determines the course of your life. You may work grudgingly or you may work gratefully; you may work as a human or you may work as a robot. There is no work so rude that you may not exalt in it; no work so demeaning that you cannot breathe soul into it; no work so dull that you may not enliven it.

—Og Mandino

Og Mandino had a terrible time coping with his mother's untimely death. Her dream that her son would be a great writer was shattered. Instead of going to college, he went to work in a paper factory and then joined the US Army Air Corps. After the war and months of unemployment, he secured a life insurance sales job. The ensuing ten years, being married with a daughter and struggling to sell insurance, pushed him deeper and deeper into debt – in his own words, 'I began to do what so many frustrated individuals still do today, to hide from their problems.'

The long days of work ended in a bar for a drink. Soon, his drink quota became two, then four, then six. He became an alcoholic, and his family left him. After two years of odd jobs, he decided to take his life. He went to buy a gun but was unable to muster enough guts to do it, and he landed himself in a library. Wandering aimlessly in the library, he gravitated towards the shelf containing self-help, success, and motivational books. He picked several books and started reading for answers on where he had gone wrong. Then he visited many libraries across the country, reading hundreds of books on success. He slowly kicked the drinking habit. The Napoleon Hill and W. Clement Stone book *Success through a Positive Mental Attitude* literally changed his life. About it, Mandino said, 'I am so impressed with Stone's philosophy of success that one must be prepared to pay a price in order to achieve any worthwhile goals.'

He went to work for Stone as an insurance salesman, got remarried, and got promoted to sales manager within one year. When he took to writing, he was assigned to the sales promotion department. He managed to turn the in-house magazine, *Success Unlimited*, into a national magazine, growing the staff from two to sixty-two and attaining a circulation of 250,000 copies. For one particular issue of the magazine, he needed one more article to fill the space. He decided to run an article on the horrible automobile accident of Ben Hogan, one of the greatest, most legendary golfers in history. A New York publisher enjoyed the article featuring Ben Hogan's dramatic recovery, which involved him proving doctors wrong that he would not walk again and then going on to win the National Open Golf Tournament. The publisher wrote to Mandino, offering to publish his book if he decided to write one. What a great opening for a new destiny to unfold.

Eighteen months later, *The Greatest Salesman in the World* was published, with five thousand copies in print. The fate of the book was rewritten when the cofounder of Amway, Richard DeVos, endorsed the book at a convention. In the next few years after that, the total sales of the book reached 350,000 copies. Even today, it continues to sell more than 100,000 copies a month. If Mandino had successfully taken his life, the world would have lost his internationally acclaimed classic, which has outsold its competition. It is ranked the number-one, all-time-best inspiration and sales book ever written, with more than fourteen million copies sold.

You may have experienced people laughing at an idea of yours. You may have felt uneasy, embarrassed, and disappointed. Any fool can do this to you. You can hardly find people who are able to give positive feedback or encouragement. The world needs Dream Walkers who can think boldly and be visionaries. The world needs dreamers who achieve the 'impossible' – who stay focused when others leave because they think something is truly impossible.

Now, consider that, for years, the world believed man could never run a mile in four minutes. In 1945, Sydney Wooderson set a record of 4 minutes 4.2 seconds, which lasted for nine years. But one man, Roger Bannister, did what the world thought was impossible on 6 May 1954, in 3 minutes 59.4 seconds. As part of his training, he set out to relentlessly visualize the achievement in order to create a sense of certainty in his mind and body. Just forty-six days later, on 21 June in Turku, Finland, Bannister's record was broken by his rival John Landy with a time of 3 minutes 57.9 seconds. How could the next guy do within forty-six days what the world thought was impossible for years? As A. P. J. Abdul Kalam said, 'The mind is unbelievably elastic. It can expand as much as you let it, and once it opens up, there are no barriers – the belief in yourself that comes as a result is something no one can take away from you.'

Dream Walkers are ordinary people who achieve the extraordinary. You, too, can join this league. Let us look at some ordinary people who are living extraordinary lives despite the calamities and obstacles they have faced. They never let anything deter them from achieving their goals.

MELISSA STOCKWELL

Twenty-four-year-old Melissa Stockwell was an athlete and an aspiring young gymnast who dreamed of the Olympics. On 13 April 2004, a roadside explosion in a convoy on the streets of Iran shattered her dreams and made her a Purple Heart recipient with the US Army. Initially, she just felt thankful to have her life. Then endless questions came to her; how life would move on was difficult to answer.

Over many surgeries, days turned into weeks, and weeks turned into months. On the fifty-second day, she took her first step on the prosthetic leg. This reassured her that she could walk and be independent. She began to swim at Walter Reed National Military Medical Center as part of her physical therapy.

Eventually, she changed her game plan and trained to compete in the 2008 Summer Paralympic Games for the US team, in which she became the record holder for the one-hundred-metre butterfly and the one-hundred-metre freestyle. She gained national attention when she became the face of the Hartford US Paralympics partnership ad campaign. 'I can really do anything I want to do, missing leg or not,' she says. The 2008 Beijing Summer Paralympic Games came and went. She got no medals. But she said, 'I learned in life sometimes the journey is more important than the destination.' Her mind is now focused on the 2016 Summer Paralympic Games in Rio de Janeiro, Brazil, where the paratriathlon event will make its debut.

Hers is a beautiful story of a Dream Walker, in a world of Dream Talkers, who lives believing, as Helen Keller said, 'Optimism is the faith that leads to achievement. Nothing can be done without hope or confidence.'

RICHARD BRANSON

Richard Branson has dyslexia, a disorder that makes it difficult to learn to read words, letters, and other symbols. He was a bad student who got bad marks and did poorly on standard tests. Today, he is the fourth-richest man in the United Kingdom, and he uses the power of his personality to drive him to success.

Virgin, his brand, is one of the world's most irresistible brands, and it has expanded into many diverse sectors, from travel to telecommunications, health to banking, and music to leisure. There are now more than one hundred Virgin companies worldwide, employing approximately sixty thousand people in more than fifty countries. Since Branson founded Virgin Atlantic in 1984, it has established itself as a leading global airline. Branson has become the only person to build US$8 billion companies in eight different sectors.

Branson has challenged himself with many record-breaking adventures, including the fastest-ever Atlantic Ocean crossing, a series of hot-air-balloon adventures, and kite surfing across the English Channel. Branson has dreamed of space travel since he watched the moon landings on TV, and he registered the *Virgin Galactic* name in 1999. Testing for commercial space services is underway, with Branson planning to join his family on the first space flight.

He is also a record breaker online, voted the UK's number-one Twitter user, the world's most social CEO, and the world's most followed person on LinkedIn. Branson maintains a daily blog on Virgin's website, discussing everything from entrepreneurship, to conservation and sustainability, to travel, music, and humour. He has more than 11.5 million followers across five social networks. Branson was awarded a knighthood in 1999 for services to entrepreneurship.

Sir Richard Branson, a Dream Walker, never let his dyslexia stop him from living his dreams. He says, 'The best way of learning about anything is by doing.'

OPRAH WINFREY

An inspiring, rich, and successful African American woman, Oprah Winfrey was raped when she was nine by her nineteen-year-old cousin, who was babysitting her. She was sexually abused by her cousin, a family friend, her mother's boyfriend, and her uncle. At the age of thirteen, Winfrey ran away from home, and delivered a child at the age of fourteen.

She did not come from a rich or even middle-class family. She was born into an economically troubled neighbourhood and raised by a single teenaged mother. But Winfrey's past didn't stop her from becoming the force she is today. She excelled as a student in high school and won an oratory contest, which secured her full scholarship to college. During high school, Winfrey wasn't certain what she wanted to do; however, she knew she wanted to do something with speaking or drama.

She was offered a job just a few months before her graduation. She had to choose between the job and graduation. She decided to choose the job, as the offer was very tempting. At the job, she wasn't a very good reporter and was fired shortly thereafter. Winfrey's boss set her up as a talk show host on a morning talk show called *People Are Talking*. After the show, Winfrey realized this was what she wanted to do for the rest of her life. As Tony Robbins says, it was during that moment of decision her destiny was shaped. Winfrey worked on strengthening the talk show for seven years before deciding to move on.

In 1981, Winfrey sent recorded tapes of her talk show to *A.M. Chicago*. They offered her a job. On 8 September 1986, the show was broadcasted nationally with a change of name to *The Oprah Winfrey Show*. The rest is history, with the show winning several prestigious awards. She inspired millions, helped thousands lead better lives, and paved the way for others to become successful. Her show focused on gender inequality, racism, poverty, and other issues affecting the general public.

Winfrey went on to receive a lifetime achievement award from the National Academy of Television Arts and Sciences in 1998. Then, in 2011, she received a Jean Hersholt Humanitarian Award from the Academy of Motion Picture Arts and Sciences. Over the years, life has been her great teacher.

Let us study some of her thoughts.

ON GRATITUDE

'If you concentrate on what you have, you will always end up having more. If you focus on what you don't have, you will never, ever have enough.'

Early in the morning, just before the benign light breaks the dawn, you will notice silence all around you. As the first ray of light bursts through the sky, silent birds start chirping joyfully to welcome the dawn of another day, which binds us with nature. But many people start the day by hammering the clock to silence, rushing to a quick shower, and frantically beating the jam to be in the office. Why not, for a change, wake up thirty minutes earlier and start the day on a different note? Just enjoy the day by expressing gratitude for all the abundance in your life. Thank your loved ones; thank your friends; thank your healthy body; thank nature for all its beauty; just thank all those you wish to thank. Focus on what you have; it will lead to abundance in all areas and the strength to persevere and move forward.

ON FAILURE

In her 2013 Harvard University commencement speech, Winfrey said, 'There is no such thing as failure. Failure is just life trying to move us in another direction.'

As she says, there is no such thing as failure. It just means you did not get the result you expected. Just change your strategy or have a new game plan and move ahead with new vigour. Don't call it *failure*; call it an *unexpected result* to learn from and rectify. Write in your journal. Have a conversation with yourself. Do some deep thinking. Analyse and evaluate what went wrong and what you need to change or rectify to get the desired result. When you write in a journal, the record will come in handy to reveal what you have learned and how to solve a similar problem in the future.

ON RESPECT

'I don't yell at people, I don't mistreat people. I don't talk down to people, so no one else in this building, in this vicinity, has the right to do it.'

Learn to love yourself. When you love yourself, you will learn to love people. Learn to respect people. Learn to treat people well. People love to be respected and treated well. When you love, respect, and treat people well, the same will come to you in abundance. Learn to forgive people. Not forgiving people is a heavy load to carry through life. Why should you burden yourself with something unproductive that zaps your energy? The minute you forgive, your life is energized. Just bear in mind whatever you sow, you reap.

ON PASSION

'Everybody has a calling. And your real job in life is to figure out as soon as possible what that is, who you were meant to be, and to begin to honor that in the best way possible for yourself.'

Deep inside, you may have a burning desire to achieve something you are passionate about that might be asleep. You might not have awakened the sleeping giant, or you might not have enough inspiration to awaken it. People around you could be stumbling blocks. Learn to look deep inside you; you will identify it. Believe it. Nurture it. Live it.

ON ACCOUNTABILITY

'You are responsible for your life. If you're sitting around waiting on somebody to save you, to fix you, to even help you, you are wasting your time. Only you have the power to move your life forward.'

The cardinal rule you must bear in mind is you are responsible for your life. Stop blaming others for your setbacks and unsatisfactory results. Stop wasting your time sitting around and waiting for help. If someone lends a hand to pull you up, just receive it, but move ahead with your plan.

ALBERT EINSTEIN

Nobel Prize winner in physics Albert Einstein did not speak until he was four or read until he was seven. His parents and teachers thought he was mentally handicapped. Many people believed Einstein would never succeed at anything.

Einstein went on to become a professor at the University of Zürich and, later, a professor of theoretical physics in Prague. Einstein published more than 300 scientific papers, along with more than 150 nonscientific works. He then proved to all the doubting, ridiculing scientists throughout the world that he did have a brilliant mind by winning the Nobel Prize in 1921. Einstein's intellectual achievements and originality have made the word *Einstein* synonymous with *genius*. What a beautiful saying by Albert Einstein: 'Everyone is a genius.'

Einstein went on to say that 'doing the same thing over and over again and expecting different results' is insanity.

Why not ask yourself what you can do differently starting today to get new results? Sixty thousand thoughts cross your mind daily. Your mood can constantly swing, from happy to unhappy or from joyful to sad. Yesterday, you could have been in the most joyful mood, but today, things could have changed to put you in a bad mood. This afternoon, things could change again to put you on top of the world. Are you going to live a roller-coaster life or seize the moment and live the life of your choice? You can decide how you are going to respond to every situation. You are responsible and accountable for all decisions you make regarding your life. As Roger Dawson said, 'The most self-destructive thought that any person can have is thinking that he or she is not in control of his or her life.'

You are a genius. You have the most powerful brain, you are unique, you are special, and you are different. I could go on and on. Don't wait for others to solve your problems or hand you opportunities on a platter. Everybody has his or her own set of problems to solve. Be proactive, seize the moment, make decisions, and move. What you sow, you reap. What they sow, they reap. Sowing and reaping are your birthright. Just decide what you want to sow, and reap it.

POWER THOUGHTS 7

Every day, I am up early in the morning to enjoy the break of light and the silence. I welcome with joy the dawn of another day that binds me with nature. I start the day with quality time with myself. I express gratitude for the abundance I enjoy in my life by saying thank you. I thank my loved ones, I thank my friends, I thank my healthy body, I thank nature for its beauty – just everything and everyone I wish to thank. When I focus on what I have, it leads to abundance in all areas of my life and to the strength to persevere and move forward.

I greet this day with love in my heart. I love myself. I love every person, I respect every person, and I treat every person well. I love to be respected and treated well, in the same way every person loves to be respected and treated well. When I do this, the same respect and good treatment comes to me in abundance.

I look deep inside me to identify what I am passionate about. I identify it. Believe it. Nurture it. Live it.

I am responsible for my life. I do not blame others for my setbacks and unsatisfactory results. I am in control of my life.

I know every day, sixty thousand thoughts cross my mind. I am in control of my life. I select the thoughts I want to nurture. I nurture the thoughts I have selected.

I am a genius. I have the most powerful brain, I am unique, I am special, and I am different. I seize the moment, I make decisions, and I move on to live my dreams. I am proactive. I enjoy the bountiful.

CHAPTER 8

Friends

We are what we repeatedly do. Excellence, then, is not an act, but a habit.

—Aristotle

In the course of our lives, we meet many people. Some become good friends, some are okay friends, some are acquaintances, and many we just meet and say hi and bye to. Some we meet every day, some we meet regularly, some we meet occasionally, some we meet at social functions, and some we hardly meet. Some we love, some we respect, some we adore, some we admire, some we learn from, some we follow, and many just pass through our lives. Who is a true friend? Famous painter and artist Vincent van Gogh said, 'Close friends are truly life's treasures. Sometimes they know us better than we know ourselves. With gentle honesty, they are there to guide and support us, to share our laughter and our tears. Their presence reminds us that we are never really alone.'

Let me also share with you what the great poet Ralph Waldo Emerson had to say about friendship: 'The glory of friendship is not the outstretched hand, not the kindly smile, nor the joy of companionship; it is the spiritual inspiration that comes to one when you discover that someone else believes in you and is willing to trust you with a friendship.'

So when we put their interpretations together, it means a true friend is someone who really knows us, guides and supports us, shares our laughter and our tears, believes in us, and lets us not feel lonely. You could agree or disagree with their interpretation. You have the right to decide on your own interpretation. But bear in mind our success is very much dependent on the friends we are surrounded by. So be selective; be choosy with the kind of people you want to associate with for your success. If you want your dreams to happen, then be among people who are like-minded.

I would like to share with you the inspirational stories of some fine gentlemen whom I was fortunate to meet in different phases of my life. They all come from different walks of life and backgrounds. They pursued their dreams relentlessly with passion, perseverance, and perspective. They are all Dream Walkers who worked relentlessly to reach their goals.

My education started in a Christian missionary school from preschool. We were blessed with excellent teachers who were dedicated to their profession. To ensure that I attained good results, my parents sent me to private tutors. My friendship with Elanko, who also attended the classes, continued in my working world. Let me share the story of this teacher-cum-ice cream seller who became an entrepreneur, a highly motivated person who had to settle for becoming a trained school teacher due to his family's financial constraints.

Elanko started his career as a teacher in a Tamil school. The desire to succeed financially kept burning deep inside him. He did not sit and wait for the opportunity; as the saying goes, 'Don't wait for the ship to sail in; swim out to it.' After work, he sold general insurance and ventured into ice cream wholesaling. His discipline made him save diligently for future opportunities. The next opportunity that knocked on his door was venturing into a logistics business. As Tony Robbins says, his destiny was shaped in the moments of that decision. Then he left teaching and focused on developing the logistics business.

Elanko believed in the following philosophy: 'The customers are our priority; we give them our best service at all times.' This philosophy has rewarded him handsomely. Today, he manages a fleet of lorries, including special-purpose low loaders. He has also ventured into warehouse management, which is synergistic with his existing business. He has expanded and built a second warehouse to cater to his customers' needs. He fulfilled his desire to attain a degree in the midst of his business commitments. His prosperity has led to his generous support of spiritual and community responsibilities. He is a true Dream Walker living his dream.

When I was a student pursuing my degree in Chennai, India, I joined a group of students to rent a flat close to our college. We even employed a cook to dish out some fine food for us. It was a great experience, venturing out on our own from the secure environment of a hostel. Student life was interesting but challenging, as we had to live on a tight budget to make ends meet living far away from home. It was a wonderful experience, sharing a flat with strangers who became close friends. One of the friends who shared the flat was a bachelor of science graduate from the prestigious Loyola College. He was a wonderful person, creating a lively atmosphere with his witty jokes and dramatic acts. His dream was to pursue a degree in medical science to become a medical doctor. Vain attempts to secure a medical seat didn't deter him from his desire to succeed.

His story reminds me of the great leader A. P. J. Abdul Kalam, the ninth president of India. Kalam had a dream to be a pilot – an Indian Air Force pilot. He was one among the twenty-five shortlisted candidates invited to attend an interview in Delhi. His dream was shattered when he stood eighth and just missed it by a notch. This deeply disturbed him; he had to change plans and reassess his priorities. He decided to go to Rishikesh and take a dip in the Ganges. He then noticed the Divine Life Society ashram and walked up to the ashram. He was granted an audience with the founder, Swami Sivananda. The Swamiji said to him, 'Accept your destiny and go ahead with your life. You are not destined to become an air force pilot. What you are destined to become is not revealed now but it is predetermined. Forget this failure, as it was essential to lead you to your destined path. Search, instead, for the true purpose of your existence. ... Surrender yourself to the wish of God.'

On his return to Delhi, an appointment as senior scientific assistant with the Ministry of Defence was waiting for him. This is how he started his career, as destined. One failure led him to success as one of the most distinguished scientists of India. He then went on to play a pivotal role in the development and launch of a satellite launch vehicle and Rohini satellite, respectively.

Now let us go into the story of our hero S. Kolandaisamy, who is fondly called Samy. Samy decided to return to Malaysia to seek employment. He had to settle for a low-paying job and take up a second job to supplement his income. On my return, I joined an engineering company as purchasing assistant. My friend joined the same company in the foundry division. After a hard day's work, he would not return home and rest on his laurels, waiting for something to drop from the sky. He would travel in his two-wheeler, soliciting prospective clients for the life insurance business he was pursuing part-time. Like Ali, he hated every minute of travelling, but he said to himself, *Don't quit. Suffer now and live the rest of your life as a champion.* He did not resign and accept it as his fate. He believed that he could change anything if he just believed in himself and pursued his dream. He upgraded his knowledge and skills through the trainings and seminars the company and industry provided. He pursued acquiring the professional qualification the life insurance industry offered.

Today, he holds a string of qualifications – BSc, LUTCF, FChFP, RFP, and FNAMLIFA – and the position of senior group sales manager with an established life insurance company, living his dream. As Abdul Kalam said, 'His dreams were not those that he saw in his sleep; they were the ones that never let him sleep.' Today, his credentials are numerous, and he is a speaker for the Asia Pacific Life Insurance Council. He is a staunch believer in the whole-man concept advocated by Million Dollar Round Table (MDRT) focusing on financial, social, mental, physical, and spiritual success. He is a practitioner of Zig Ziglar's powerful words: 'If you help enough people get what they want you get anything that you want.' S. K. Samy, who achieved his financial freedom shared, 'I am happy where I am and I thank the Almighty for His blessings.'

In my quest to upgrade myself, I enrolled in a master's program in business administration with a British university's distance-learning program. I consider myself fortunate to have got the friendship of two gentlemen, Mogan and Tamil who were successful in their own ways. The three of us formed a group study team. We devoted the weekends to group study at our friend Tamil's office. We even shared a room in Singapore when sitting for our examination.

Mogan comes from an ordinary and hardworking family. He successfully graduated from a local university. When he decided to pursue his master's, he was working as a manager with an established international float-glass manufacturing company. He believed in the philosophy you can make a mark working in one industry. On completion of his master's degree, Mogan pursued working in a different glass-related industry. He moved up the corporate ladder of the company swiftly through passion, dedication, and commitment. He is currently the chief executive officer of an established international glass-container manufacturing company. By helping his workers, staff, management, directors, and shareholders achieve their dreams, Mogan Muniandy, a Dream Walker, has been able to realize his dreams. Mogan shares this golden saying with his staff: 'Believe in yourself, and always strive for excellence.'

Let me share with you about my other friend, Tamil, who was the branch manager of an international pharmaceutical distributor. He was a very ambitious person in pursuit of his dream. He resigned and set up his own group of pharmacies. This also provided him the opportunity to diversify into lucrative commercial ventures. The business boomed and gave him handsome returns. But this was short-lived, as he was overzealous and made some irrevocable, blatant mistakes and blunders. It was a very testing time for him. He had to overcome the pressing financial loss and mental agony. He never let failures dampen his spirits. He believed in himself. He knew he could bounce back.

At this point in time, a friend introduced him to another business opportunity called *network marketing*. As Robert Kiyosaki said, 'A network marketing system, a system I often call a personal franchise, is a very democratic way of wealth creation.' Tamil was one who never believed in network marketing. His destiny was shaped when he decided to reevaluate his path and take a shot at this business concept. As he was getting into the system, a brand-new company with a similar concept knocked on his door. Tamil decided this was the opportunity he was waiting for. As Tony Robbins says, it was in his moments of decision his destiny was shaped.

Let me go back a little. Tamil came from a very ordinary family. His parents were rubber tappers. He started his education in a Tamil estate school. During his free time, he used to follow his mother to tap rubber trees. He said proudly, 'I usually complete the task much faster than the others.' He was very proud of his ability. He excelled in his studies and believed in the infinite potential within the fortress of his mind. He got an admission into the engineering faculty of the University of Malaya. He was an outstanding student, he was very active in debate and public speaking, and he excelled as a student union leader and activist. During a student clash with the police, he was arrested and placed under police detention. He was then expelled from the university but given a second lease on life to pursue a degree in pharmacy at Universiti Sains, Penang. This is the story of his pharmaceutical degree.

Tamil is an excellent speaker, motivator, and go-getter who strategized and moved swiftly up the ladder of success, helping his leaders and team members achieve their dreams. He travels the world promoting his company. He is a top leader with an international networking company holding the rank of Gold International Diamond. I can say with conviction that his massive success is due to him being a go-getter, working tirelessly, helping people achieve their dreams, and, in the process, achieving his dreams.

My passion and commitment to community service got me the friendships of some fine gentlemen. One of them is Anga. He was born into a family of seven. His parents were tappers at a rubber plantation. They went to work in the wee hours of the morning, leaving the children at home. His days started differently than most students' days. He would gather the sludge rubber before the long walk to school as his contribution to the family kitty. His responsibilities did not end then; cleaning the rubber cups after school was another daily chore. A hearty meal was rare; most times, rice with curry was his main and staple meal. During very difficult times, wheat *thosai* (Indian pancakes) and tapioca served as main staple food. The long and lonely three-kilometre walk with his brother through rows of neatly lined rubber trees and a narrow and uneven road surfaced with gravel and mud was challenging and time consuming. The walk got frustrating, with potholes during the rainy season and dust during the dry season. Electricity was a luxury, and they had to do good with kerosene lamps.

He was not an outstanding student, but he cleared the hurdles through sheer hard work. He cleared his public examination at the age of fifteen and was promoted to the higher secondary. He had a burning desire to do well in life. He was well aware that his only ray of hope to succeed in life was education. To do well in the public examination, he had to work very hard and produce outstanding results to get admission into his dream medical faculty of the local university. As Tony Robbins said, 'It is in your moments of decision your destiny is shaped.'

A decision he made at this juncture literally changed his life. He decided to take massive action and to act as if it was impossible to fail. He decided to claim his birthright and not accept a life of mediocrity. He decided not to be the prisoner of his past but to be the architect of his future. He decided that he had to study a minimum of six hours after school and ten to twelve hours during holidays to achieve his dream. He had to burn the midnight oil to achieve his dream. It was not easy but definitely possible. With an environment not conducive for studying, but a burning desire, faith, perseverance, ambition, dedication, and hard work, he was able to cross the next major examinations with flying colours. This earned him a place in the medical faculty of the premier Malaya university. He pursued his postgraduate work in general surgery and plastic surgery in 1984 and 1988, respectively. The reality of life is this: people love to have the dream look of their choice. He makes their dreams reality. Anga subscribes to this reality statement by Zig Ziglar: 'If you help enough people get what they want you get anything that you want.'

Anga is also a specialist in arteriovenous fistula, or *AV fistula*. This is a surgically modified blood vessel created by connecting an artery to a vein. The fistula will usually be created in a wrist and upper-arm surgery for kidney dialysis patients. He has a very high success rate for this surgery nationwide.

Angamuthu is a petit and simple person with a big heart. He gives back to society through nongovernmental organizations, such as the Educational, Welfare and Research Foundation (EWRF), an Indian-based organization. As a gesture of his appreciation for the financial assistance given to him during his college days, he joined Rotary and serves the needy. The hospice centre supported by his Rotary club is housed in his building. He travels to the Philippines to perform free cleft surgeries for the poor and needy as an ongoing international Rotary service project with clubs in the Philippines. Angamuthu is a classic example of a Dream Walker in a world of Dream Talkers. He always says, 'My success is due to the massive action I took day in and day out, just putting in minimum hours a day to study.'

Now let me share about the next gentleman I met by chance. When his chauffeur wanted to manage a cafeteria for the workers of a power station that was under construction, he approached me for help to set up the outlet. He then told me, 'I would like you to meet my boss.' I went to meet his boss – a simple, down-to-earth, lovable person – in Kuala Lumpur. We discussed how to make the project a success. Then he took time off from his busy schedule to visit the site to personally assess the viability and discuss it further. He genuinely wanted to help his employee succeed in the business.

This is how I got acquainted with a highly reputable player in structural design, fabrication, and erection of steel structures twelve years ago, who is fondly called A. K. His company has commissioned the steel structures for some of the tallest and largest buildings in the world. He was involved in the construction of steel structures of the then-tallest buildings in the world: the Petronas Twin Towers in Malaysia and Burj Khalifa in the Middle East. The company has completed hundreds of landmark projects in Malaysia, Singapore, the Philippines, Indonesia, Thailand, Hong Kong, India, and the Middle East.

His ambition to be a medical doctor did not materialise due to financial constraints. I think he took the path Swami Sivananda shared with Abdul Kalam. He accepted his destiny – that he was not destined to become a doctor. What he was destined to become was not revealed then but was predetermined. He forgot that setback, as it was essential to lead to his destined path. He searched, instead, for the true purpose of his existence: to surrender himself to the wish of God. He sailed back to Malaysia from India, started working as a printing machine operator, and then joined the life insurance industry as a salesman.

A novice to the engineering field became a risk taker when he grabbed the first opportunity, which came by accident, to venture into the construction industry through a Japanese megaproject in Malaysia called *Dayabumi*. This fitted perfectly with what Tony Robbins has shared: 'It is in your moments of decision your destiny is shaped.' This project opened A. K.'s mind; as Abdul Kalam said, 'The mind is unbelievably elastic. It can expand as much as you let it, and once it opens up, there are no barriers – the belief in yourself that comes as a result is something no one can take away from you.'

Tan Sri A. K. Nathan, executive chairman and group managing director of Eversendai, had a humble beginning in 1984. Through hard work, persistence, perseverance, and an expanded mind, he steered the company from a one-man operation to a corporate giant with more than six thousand employees. Today, Eversendai is one of the largest steel contractors in the Middle East and one of the most sought-after structural-steel enterprises in the world.

When I completed this chapter, I sat down to enjoy my daily inspiration by Robin Sharma: 'The people who get on in life are those who dream big dreams and then take whatever risks are necessary to bring their vision to life. They face their fears directly, get into the game and live their days with courage. They break through their fear doors, no matter how scared they feel. It's better to be a lion for a day than a sheep all your life.' I just love this saying by Robin Sharma. What really fascinates me is this gentleman's level of commitment to ensure that his employee who was venturing into the business world succeeded. Not many people will go the extra mile to ensure others succeed. This a beautiful lesson for all of us to learn from.

These friends of mine are Dream Walkers who took massive actions to succeed. They are ordinary people like you and me who did the extraordinary. As Zig Ziglar said, they helped others get what they wanted, and in return, they got what they wanted. They had their fair share of unsatisfactory results and setbacks. They did not let the unsatisfactory results and setbacks dampen their spirits. They used their unsatisfactory results and setbacks as trampolines to bounce back as lessons for success. You will never go wrong helping people get what they want because, in return, you will get whatever you want. I honestly believe life is a treasure chest with the finest jewels and ornaments to be discovered and enjoyed.

POWER THOUGHTS 8

I am selective. I choose the people I want to be associated with. For my dreams to happen, I associate with like-minded people.

I believe in myself. I do not allow unsatisfactory results and setbacks to dampen my spirit. I use the lessons learned from unsatisfactory results and setbacks as a trampoline to bounce back and succeed. I always strive for excellence.

I am a go-getter. I believe in helping others achieve their dreams, and in the process, I achieve my dreams.

I dream big dreams. I take whatever risks necessary to bring my vision to life. I face my fears directly. I live my days with courage. I would rather be a lion for a day than a sheep all my life.

CHAPTER 9

Passion

For him who has conquered the mind, the mind is the
best of friends; but for one who has failed to do so, his
mind will remain the greatest enemy.

—Bhagavad Gita

We are all gifted with some special talents. Sometimes, we discover them by accident. Sometimes, others discover them and encourage us to develop them. Many a time, we live our lives without discovering them. So pursue your special talents, your core competencies, and the genius in you. Master them, claim what is your birthright, and live like the great people in this book. Never let others decide your dreams and your fate.

I was just slouched in my chair, relaxed with a cup of tea, a novice and a layman to music, mesmerized, when Ludwig van Beethoven's Ninth Symphony, the most glorious and jubilant masterpiece, with Riccardo Muti and the Chicago Symphony Orchestra and Chorus, burst with brooding power and kinetic energy and culminated in the exultant hymn 'Ode to Joy'. It's an exhilarating testament to the human spirit and was performed on 7 May 2015, its anniversary.

It is impossible to think that Beethoven was deaf and could not hear his own masterpiece when he shared it with the world on 7 May 1824.

Ludwig van Beethoven remains one of the world's most famous and influential composers of classical music. His music has been played all over the world for more than two hundred years. He only wrote nine symphonies, as compared to Haydn and Mozart, who, combined, wrote more than 150 symphonies. It took Beethoven twenty-five years to compose all nine symphonies. He was very meticulous about his work, often reworking it many times over. He could not hear his own music, but he composed all his nine symphonies. His efforts made a profound impact on the world. After two hundred years, orchestras all over the world are playing his symphonies, people are buying them on CDs, and millions of people are listening to them.

Malcolm Gladwell said you can master anything – be it music, painting, or sports – if you can achieve ten thousand hours of practice, but some dispute this. If Beethoven had practised just more than an hour a day in twenty-five years, he would have surpassed ten thousand hours. Beethoven is one of the world's most famous and influential composers of classical music, so he definitely did far better than that. Practice makes perfect. If you want to be the best, just keep practising and perfecting.

Beethoven lived as a Dream Walker in a world dominated by Dream Talkers, who give reasons for all they can't do. If he had been a Dream Talker, he would have given his deafness as a reason he couldn't compose, and the world would not know Beethoven or his music.

I was deep in thought over an issue that was disturbing me when the upbeat music of 'Jai Ho' rejuvenated and rekindled my spirit and, within a split second, changed my mood to one of joy. I started tapping the table with my fingers and the floor with my feet to the beat, though I did not understand the Hindi lyrics. Music is universal. The song 'Jai Ho [Victory to Thee]', composed by A. R. Rahman, was destined to win awards. It received universally favourable reviews from music critics.

The Indian composer, singer, songwriter, record producer, music director, arranger, entrepreneur, philanthropist, and conductor A. R. Rahman, born A. S. Dileep Kumar, is nicknamed the *Mozart of Madras* and *Isai Puzal* ('Music Storm'). He has mastered the keyboard, piano, synthesizer, harmonium, and guitar. He also plays the drums, accordion, goblet drum, and concert harp. His works are notable for integrating Eastern classical music with electronic music sounds, world music genres, and traditional orchestral arrangements. He says, 'For me, there is no day or night for music. I often work through the night – without phone calls disturbing me.'

Just one movie, *Slumdog Millionaire*, directed by Danny Boyle, bagged A. R. Rahman several international awards. The 2008 British-Indian drama film won him two prestigious Academy Awards, one Golden Globe Award, two Grammy Awards, and a BAFTA in 2009. Rahman became the first Asian person to receive three Oscar nominations and win two Oscars in the same year. He was the third Asian person to win two Academy Awards. The Academy Award winner shares, 'Success comes to those who dedicate everything to their passion in life. To be successful, it is also very important to be humble and never let fame or money travel to your head.'

Rahman started his career composing musical scores for television, advertisements, and documentaries. Rahman debuted as a film composer when popular Tamil director Mani Ratnam approached him to score the movie *Roja*, which won him the National Film Award for best music direction. The award was the first for a debut music director.

Rahman – the son of R. K. Shekhar, a conductor and composer of Tamil and Malayalam songs – started learning piano when he was only four years old. He lost his father when he was only nine, and family responsibilities fell on his shoulders at a very tender age. The family survived on a rental income from musical instruments left behind by his father. The award winner has said, 'Each one of us has our own evolution of life, and each one of us goes through different tests which are unique and challenging. But certain things are common. And we do learn things from each other's experience. On a spiritual journey, we all have the same destination.' Rahman's victory mantra involves having big dreams, connecting with his audience by listening more, and delivering with passion. He believes in practise, practise, practise!

In 2015, New Delhi Television (NDTV) honoured twenty-five Indians as the greatest living Indian legends. Rahman was one of the recipients of the honour. The selections were made by eminent Indians and an online poll of people of Indian origin who excelled in their specific discipline in India and globally. You could say Beethoven and Rahman were born with talent. You could be true, but they definitely could not have become great musicians, with outstanding performances, without incredible discipline and hard work.

Now let me share what I liked as a kid. Like all children, I loved watching cartoons. One of them was Mickey Mouse – an enjoyable, energetic character, with his unique voice and entertaining actions attracting children and adults of all ages and races across the globe and making them laugh. Many people can recall fond memories of spending time with their children watching these cartoons. This character, Mickey, in red velvet pants, was created by Walt Disney in 1928. He thought him up on a train ride back from New York to Los Angeles with his wife after a business meeting where he lost the copyright of his cartoon character Oswald the Rabbit.

Walt Disney, the recipient of twenty-six Academy Awards, the most for an individual in Academy Awards history, was once fired for 'lack of imagination'. His first animation company went bankrupt. Legend has it that he got his financing for creating Disney World after being turned down 302 times. His ingredients for success were vision, planning, hard work, and the star Mickey Mouse, which he created.

As a parent in the 1930s, he had a dream to 'make a park for kids, a place scaled down to kid size'. In 1940, he revealed his plan. In 1948, he shared his concept with his friends. In 1952, he decided on the name *Disneyland*. His brother, the financial head of their studio, was against the project. Bankers and the amusement industry predicted the project would be a sure failure. But Walt Disney stood his ground and believed in his dream. Walt Disney believed in a Henry Ward Beecher quote: 'Your best success comes after your greatest disappointment.'

Disneyland opened on 17 July 1955; within seven weeks, a million visitors made a beeline for Disneyland, making it the biggest tourist attraction in the United States. Attendance and guest spending surpassed predictions by 50 and 30 per cent, respectively. Once again, Walt Disney proved his critics wrong. The first time he proved critics wrong was when *Snow White and the Seven Dwarfs* was released in 1938, it earned US$8 million, and it was the highest grossing movie that year, though critics predicted it would be a disaster.

People can say what they want; Walt Disney would not have made history if he had heeded the critics' predictions. People called him a workaholic; let it be so, but he was driven by his dreams. His winning mantra was this: 'Everybody can make their dreams come true. It takes a dream – faith in it – and hard work. But that's not quite true because it's so much fun you hardly realize its work.'

As Walt Disney said, if you enjoy doing a job, then it is not hard work but sheer fun. If you dread doing it, then it is definitely hard work. Life is a beautiful gift to enjoy. Why do things you dislike or you dread doing? Why not choose to do the things you like and do them with passion? You have another option: to learn to accept whatever you are doing as something you like and enjoy. Then it will become fun. You decide the state of mind you will have while undertaking a job.

Let me share with you the success story of John Grisham. His first novel, *A Time to Kill*, is based on an actual rape case Grisham, a lawyer by profession, witnessed. The story is about a young black girl who was raped by two drunken white men from the South. The girl's father vows revenge and guns them down as they leave the courtroom. A young white lawyer, a friend of the black girl's father, decides to defend this almost impossible case. The rest of the story follows the turbulence surrounding the case.

Grisham's first book was rejected twenty-eight times before he got a yes for five thousand copies to be printed. Not many of us can take that many rejections. But Grisham decided to be different and persist. Nine of his novels have been turned into films. Grisham shares, 'I seriously doubt I would ever have written the first story had I not been a lawyer. I never dreamed of being a writer. I wrote only after witnessing a trial.' His destiny as a writer was shaped when he witnessed a trial. Currently, more than three hundred million John Grisham books are in print worldwide, and the books have been translated into forty languages. Some strange events might provide the impetus for you to follow your destiny. Keep an open mind; believe you will shape your destiny when you grab those opportunities.

The 1975 blockbuster *Jaws* saw the emergence of an award-winning director, who was the third choice to direct the film. Twenty-six-year-old Steven Spielberg wanted to quit even before production commenced. The producer had to exercise their rights to veto his departure. He was destined to direct this epic, action-packed drama based on the story of a humongous, man-eating great white shark attacking beachgoers on Amity Island, a fictional New England summer resort town. In the movie, the local police chief hunts the shark with the help of a marine biologist and professional shark hunter. The climax shows how the shark immobilizes the boat and is obliterated. A technical marvel kept the audience watching with tight fists clenching their seats. They overshot the estimated budget of US$3.5 million, reaching US$9 million. The production schedule stretched from 55 days to 159 days. On its release, the film recouped the production costs in two weeks. In 78 days, it became the highest grossing film at the North American box office.

Steven Spielberg, an amateur filmmaker from the age of ten with his father's 8-millimeter camera, lives his dream of being a film director. The award-winning director, screenwriter, and producer went on to give us enormously successful films, such as *E.T.*, *The Color Purple*, *Schindler's List*, and many more. In 1994, he got an honorary degree from the same prestigious University of Southern California film school that rejected his application twice in his teens. Spielberg is a Dream Walker who knew what he wanted in life. He pursued his dream with the zeal of a winner. The greatest honour you can ever receive is to be invited to receive an honorary degree by the same prestigious university that rejected your application, not once but twice. A Gandhi saying perfectly fits this Academy Award winner: 'A man is but a product of his thoughts. What he thinks he becomes.'

A gentle nudge from a loved one or words of appreciation will definitely go a long way to building confidence in a person. One such occurrence literally changed the fate of the book *Carrie*. Author Stephen King started work on this book, his fourth novel, while living in a trailer. After typing the first three pages on his portable typewriter, he tossed them in the garbage. His wife, Tabitha, picked up the pieces and read them. She liked them and encouraged King to continue writing. A publisher bought the book and sold the paperback rights for the novel to New American Library for US$400,000. He collected half the sum as his share and continued writing. The rest is history. He has sold more than 350 million copies of his books. He says, 'Just because something isn't happening for you right now doesn't mean that it will never happen.' Well said by the man who could have missed the boat if his wife did not pick his work out of the trash and encourage him to continue.

Tim Ferriss, an entrepreneur who ran a nutritional supplement company, says, 'Tomorrow becomes never. No matter how small the task, take the first step now.' Tim Ferriss, with partner Alicia Monti, is the 2006 *Guinness Book of World Records* holder for the most spins in one minute – thirty-seven for tango dance. He is the author of the number-one bestselling book *The 4-Hour Work Week*. He changed how many people view work and life. Twenty-six publishers rejected him before one gave him a chance. The book has been on the bestseller list for years, and it is sold all over the world and translated into many languages. He has also written *The 4-Hour Body* and *The 4-Hour Chef*. The world record holder for tango dance shares, 'There is no sure path to success, but the surest path to failure is trying to please everyone.'

We are all endowed with the same potentials as those I have shared with you. These people realized their potential, worked on it, and enjoyed success. You, too, can be a Dream Walker, enjoying your success if you realize your potential and work on it.

POWER THOUGHTS 9

I am a gifted person with special talents. I master it and claim it. It is my birthright. I decide my dreams and my fate.

I dedicate myself fully to my passion. My dedication to my passion gives me great success.

I have my own evolution in life, and I go through tests that are unique and challenging, but I have certain things in common with others. I do learn things from others.

I can have my best success come to me even after my greatest disappointment.

I am making my dreams come true. I have faith in my dreams. I work joyfully to achieve my dreams.

I believe if something isn't happening for me right now, it doesn't mean that it will never happen.

I am generous with my words of appreciation. I believe being generous with words of appreciation will build me up as a person and build up the confidence level of the person receiving the compliment.

I believe even if it is a simple task, I take the first step now itself.

I please myself first. It is my primary responsibility.

CHAPTER 10

The Best Job

Time is like a river. You cannot touch the same water twice, because the flow that has passed will never pass again. Enjoy every moment in life.

—Anonymous

Great coffee starts with great beans. Freshly ground beans, the aroma of fresh coffee, and the first sip just rocks you. I had the luxury of choosing among three Starbucks coffee outlets nested close to each other. My choice was the latest one in Johor Bahru City Centre. This outlet, housed on the third floor facing the Customs, Immigration and Quarantine Complex, was set off by a wide road. The view was excellent and exhilarating. I had a bird's-eye view of the road and the surroundings. The barista took my order: caramel macchiato and salted caramel cheesecake. I picked up my order and sat on a sofa to enjoy my breakfast and the view.

As I sipped my drink, I observed a young Indian boy and girl busily snapping selfies after coffee. Three college girls sat engrossed in their assignment while sipping their coffee. One brought her own tumbler to enjoy the Rm2 savings. Another young man was busy working at his computer with a cup of coffee. There were another two couples seated: one young and the other elderly. The furnishings were tasteful, with sofas, large tables, comfortable chairs, high stools, and raised tables to meet customers' different needs. The music was radiant for the ambience. The products for sale were well displayed. The ceiling was high and tastefully decorated. The coffee write-up on framed glass was informative – overall, a well-designed outlet. Whenever I think of coffee and good ambience, my first choice is Starbucks coffee. This prompted me to read the Starbucks story.

Howard Schultz

The childhood of future billionaire Howard Schultz was spent in a neighbourhood of low-income families. Most people there were extremely poor. That is why Schultz always knew how difficult it would be for him to break out of this poverty. However, his dream of becoming successful was stronger than any obstacle. Schultz shares, 'I saw my father losing his sense of dignity and self-respect. I am sure that this was caused mostly by the fact that he has been treated as an ordinary working man.'

At the age of twelve, he got his first job, selling newspapers, and then he went to work at a local café. When he turned sixteen, he was working at a fur store. Being physically strong, Schultz excelled at sports and was awarded an athletic scholarship to Northern Michigan University, where he received his bachelor's degree in communications in 1975. After graduation, he was a sales manager at Xerox for three years, and then he started working at a Swedish company selling home appliances, including coffee grinders, to businesses like Starbucks. Once Schultz realized that this little company was ordering way more of his coffee machines than some popular stores, he went to Seattle to meet the owners of Starbucks.

Starbucks started as a small coffee shop in Seattle, Washington, owned by three partners who met at college. These guys adored coffee and decided to share their passion by opening a small coffee shop. Their approach and enthusiasm impressed twenty-nine-year-old Schultz, who said, 'I went outside whispering to myself, Oh my gosh! what a wonderful business, what a wonderful city! I want to be a part of this.' It was love at first sight, and he literally begged for a job at Starbucks. He was offered the marketing director job at Starbucks with a salary less than half of what he was getting at that time. Howard saw great potential in the business and realized that he wanted to connect his life with Starbucks. Thus, he agreed to work there even under such inconvenient conditions.

In 1983, Schultz went to Milan and returned with latte and cappuccino recipes, which tripled Starbucks' sales over the next year. The concept of an Italian café amazed Schultz. In 1985, he proposed that the owners focus on creating a network of coffeehouses. But the CEO of Starbucks answered with a categorical no. The idea of drinking coffee literally elated Schultz, and he, being confident in his venture, resigned from the company and decided to push the envelope by opening his own business.

In 1987, Howard Schultz found out that the owners of Starbucks were going to sell their stores, the roasting factory, and their brand at a price of US$4 million, as they could not manage the business. He immediately went to his creditors for a loan. The founder of Microsoft, Bill Gates, was one of his early investors. Howard Schultz became the only owner and manager of Starbucks. In 1992, Schultz decided to make Starbucks a public company. In June of the same year, he put the company's shares on the New York Stock Exchange at the price of fourteen dollars per share. In just one day, it jumped to thirty-three dollars.

The managers of Starbucks stores from different cities reported to headquarters that customers often asked where they could buy the CDs played at the store. Starbucks immediately signed a contract with Capitol Records and, in March 1995, released their own collection of jazz and blues. On the very first day, they sold more than seventy-five thousand copies. Later, Starbucks created a subsidiary, Hear

Music, which began to release their *Blue Note* and *Blending the Blues* collections annually. Hear Music is Starbucks' retail music concept and record label.

In 1996, Starbucks' first foreign store opened in Japan. Then stores started to appear in Singapore, Korea, Taiwan, the United Kingdom, the Netherlands, Sweden, and Israel. By April 2000, there were more than 2,400 Starbucks stores in the United States and 350 stores in Europe, Asia, the Middle East, and Canada.

In early 2008, Schultz returned to Starbucks' leadership to restore the company's image. In order to save Starbucks, Schultz had to take a number of strict measures. When they needed him to restore the image, he stepped in to downsize operations to optimize costs and implement strict controls. To optimize costs, the company closed six hundred stores in 2008 and another three hundred in 2009. Schultz has shared, 'I cannot offer you any specific secret recipe for success, the perfect plan, how to reach the pinnacle of success in the business. But my own experience suggests that starting from scratch and achieving much more than what I dream about is quite possible.' Since returning to turn around the company, he comes into the office by 6.00 a.m. and stays until 7.00 p.m. As of 2014, there were 20,737 Starbucks stores in sixty-two countries generating a revenue of US$16.45 billion and net income of US$2.07 billion supported by 149,000 employees.

This is the story of Howard Schultz, whose net worth is about US$2.2 billion. He worked incredibly hard to build an empire of coffee, which he fell in love with at first sight. We can enrich our lives from lessons we can learn from this extremely resourceful person. There are always opportunities knocking on our door. If we can capitalize on them, we can reap great profits. One classic example is Starbucks' release of its own collection of jazz and blues when customers were interested in buying their CDs. They created a new business opportunity by listening to their managers' feedback.

Let us now look at some other ordinary people like you and me who worked incredibly hard to land some of the best jobs.

MICHAEL JORDAN

As a youngster, Michael Jeffrey Jordan became interested in sports. Baseball was his first love, not basketball. He was turned down to play for his varsity basketball team, as he was five feet eleven inches tall and deemed too short to play at that level. Motivated to prove his worth, he became the star of the junior varsity squad. The following summer, he grew four inches and practised tirelessly. The hard work paid off. Following high school, he earned a basketball scholarship from the University of North Carolina, where he played under legendary coach Dean Smith. In his first year, he was named ACC Freshman of the Year. He turned out to be the greatest basketball player.

He shared, 'I've missed more than nine thousand shots in my career. I've lost almost three hundred games. Twenty-six times, I've been trusted to take the game-winning shot and missed. I've failed over and over and over again in my life. And that is why I succeed.' This is something for all of us from Michael Jordan: 'I can accept failure, everyone fails at something. But I can't accept not trying.'

Phil Jackson, Jordan's long-time coach, has said, 'It was hard work that made him a legend. When Jordan first entered the league, his jump shot wasn't good enough. He spent his off season taking hundreds of jumpers a day until it was perfect.' Jackson also said, 'Jordan's defining characteristic wasn't his talent, but having the humility to know he had to work constantly to be the best.'

We look at the defining moments of successful people and throw them all the cheers and praises. Their successes are wonderful, but what preludes the successes are the hours spent behind doors practising and perfecting to become the best. They must have been painful and testing, but thinking about the defining moments got them going.

MARISSA MAYER

President and CEO of Yahoo Marissa Mayer graduated with a master's degree in computer science from Stanford. She took a gamble, pushed the envelope, and accepted an offer from a then-unknown start-up company, although she had more than a dozen lucrative job offers, because it fulfilled two of her professional principles: 'Work with the smartest people you know and seek out opportunities that push you past what you know you can accomplish.'

Marissa Mayer, a remarkable person with incredible stamina, used to work 130 hours a week, out of the 168 hours there are in a week. She used to sleep under her desk at Google. When she started her career with the company, she was Google's twentieth employee and its first female engineer. When she was thirty-seven years old, in 2012, this shy person was appointed the president and CEO of Yahoo, one of the few women in major positions of power in a male-dominated industry. Today, her personal net worth is US$380 million. Much of her personal fortune comes from what she accumulated during her thirteen years at Google. In 2014, her pay package jumped 69 per cent, to US$42 million, making her one of the highest-paid employees in the United States. Her strategy and work schedule of close to twenty-four hours a day seven days a week earned her one of the highest-paying jobs available. A systematic research-driven approach is her overall decision-making strategy.

What a remarkable leader with exceptional professional principles. If you can choose such exceptional principles, you, too, can walk in your dreams.

INDRA KRISHNAMURTHY NOOYI

Sixty-year-old president and chief financial officer of PepsiCo Indra Krishnamurthy Nooyi is one of the top female executives in the United States. She oversees PepsiCo, one of the world's largest snack-food companies, which makes and sells dozens of products, including Tropicana juices and Quaker Oats cereals. She is believed to be the highest-ranking woman of Indian heritage in Corporate America. Nooyi was ranked fourth on the *Forbes* world's 100 most powerful women list from 2008 to 2014. She was ranked the Most Powerful Woman in Business by *Fortune* magazine from 2006 to 2010. In 2009, she was named CEO of the Year by Global Supply Chain Leaders Group.

Nooyi was born into a conservative, middle-class family in Madras, India. She was a bit of a rule breaker who played on an all-girls cricket team. She played guitar on an all-female rock band while studying at Madras Christian College. After graduation, she got a master's degree at Indian Institute of Management, Calcutta. She completed her master's degree in public and private management from Yale University's School of Management in New Haven, Connecticut, in 1980. She struggled to make ends meet during her days in Yale. She had to work the graveyard overnight shift as a receptionist to make ends meet. She could not afford to buy a business suit to interview at a prestigious business consulting firm. She shared, 'My whole summer job was done in a sari because I had no money to buy clothes.'

She also shared in an interview, 'I was raising two young daughters while working seven days a week, starting work at seven and rarely leaving the office before eight at night. I took home bags of mail to read overnight and wished there were thirty-five hours a day in order to do more work.' She still takes to the stage at company functions to sing. She enjoys watching Chicago Bulls championship games to study teamwork concepts.

In the first six years, she worked on a variety of international corporate-strategy projects. In 1986, she joined Motorola as senior executive. In 1990, she joined ASEA Brown Boveri, a Swedish conglomerate, as its head of strategy. In 1994, Jack Welch of General Electric offered her a job. At the same time, PepsiCo chief executive officer Wayne Calloway also offered her a job. She recalled Wayne Calloway saying, 'Welch is the best CEO I know. ... But I have a need for someone like you, and I would make PepsiCo a special place for you.'

Indra Krishnamurthy Nooyi has five Cs for success.

- **Competence,** being a 'lifelong student', is the key to guaranteeing your personal and professional growth. Continue learning and developing your skill set, stay up to date, and become known and reputed for your chosen skill. In other words, master your chosen skill, and never shy away from knowing more.
- **Courage and confidence** will facilitate strong decision-making skills and will also let fellow colleagues know that you have an opinion and are not afraid to come forward with it. Procrastination and silence will get you nowhere in a competitive and cutthroat field.
- **Communication skills** are integral to all spheres of your professional life. Communicating effectively with your team serves to help them understand the plan of action and motivate them to meet their goals with enthusiasm and efficiency. Clear communication, which gets across your passion and vision, will also facilitate team building and will put you across as a strong leader.
- **Consistency** should guide the manner in which you conduct your business. Erratic tactics indicate an unsure mind that is not grounded and that will facilitate second-guessing from employees. Maintaining a consistent plan of action will build

your employees' confidence in you and allow them to trust your instincts.

Maintaining a personal compass will guide you in your personal life and professional life. Nooyi recommends, 'Stick to your personal sense of direction and maintain integrity despite all temptations. The act of not straying from the path of honesty will build strength of character and also strengthen your professional credibility, which is of utmost importance.'

In 2015, New Delhi Television (NDTV) honoured twenty-five Indians as the greatest living Indian legends. NDTV polled eminent Indians and online viewers to choose people of Indian origin who excelled in their specific discipline in India and globally. Indra Krishnamurthy Nooyi was one of the recipients of the honour. In her acceptance speech, she shared three lessons. She said, 'You must be a lifelong curious learner willing to totally immerse in whatever you do with the obligation to help others rise.' She is a remarkable leader living the life of a Dream Walker; she overcame the challenges faced by her conservative, middle-income family from Madras, India.

You, too, can be a Dream Walker living your dreams if you believe in yourself. Everything starts with the beliefs you harbour and nurture. Sometimes, you harbour them consciously, and sometimes, you do it unconsciously. What I have shared with you about others in this book reflects their truth and philosophy. This need not or might not be your truth. You can integrate their truth and philosophy, which are relevant to you coming up with your own truth and philosophy. This is the very idea of reading various authors' books. Once you have formed your own truth and philosophy, just anchor them with your belief, and move forward. You can make others stand aside and wonder. You can shake the world.

The truth of the matter is that you always know the right thing to do. The hard part is doing it.

—Norman Schwarzkopf

POWER THOUGHTS 10

I have the humility to work constantly to be the best.

I work with the smartest people. I seek out opportunities that push me past what I know I can accomplish.

I am courageous and confident. This facilitates the strong decision-making skills in me.

I am always acquiring good communication skills to make me a better communicator.

I stick to my personal sense of direction and maintain integrity. I stick to the path of honesty, as it will strengthen my character and my professional credibility.

I am a Dream Walker living my dreams. I realize everything starts with the beliefs I am harbouring and nurturing. I just walk it.

I have shared the difference between simply existing and truly living. You have the power to tap into this human gift and live the life of your choice.

You can choose to keep the blueprint you are holding. If you continue to do the same things, you'll get the same results; or if you change the blueprint and do new things, you'll get new results. You can push the envelope and enjoy the bounty the universe has in store for you.

We are all influenced by the strongest blueprint we hold in our mind. When we change the picture we hold in our mind, the blueprint will change and get us ready to really thrive. Change is a choice.

Discipline yourself to do what most people won't do. Then you are bound to enjoy what most people don't enjoy.

The next step is *action*. Just walk your talk.

Dear Readers,

All of us have our own remarkable success story to be shared with the world but bottled up and lying idle due to some strange reasons. I would like to hear your story and if possible share it with the world.

All you have to do is to email your remarkable story (within 200 words) to me at storythedreamwalker@gmail.com.

We will acknowledge the person sharing the story and send a complimentary copy of the book.

Printed in the United States
By Bookmasters